Small Water Enterprises in Africa
4: Ghana

Small Water Enterprises in Africa 4: Ghana

A study of small water enterprises in Accra

Ghana Project Team Leader: Kwabena Sarpong
Lead Researcher: Dr Kodjo Mensah Abrampah
Series Editors: Cyrus Njiru and Mike Smith

Water, Engineering and Development Centre
Loughborough University
2006

Water, Engineering and Development Centre,
Loughborough University,
Leicestershire, LE11 3TU, UK

© WEDC, Loughborough University, 2006

ISBN 13 Paperback: 978 1 84380 097 2
ISBN Ebook: 9781788533546
Book DOI: http://dx.doi.org/10.3362/9781788533546

A catalogue record for this book is available from the British Library.

A reference copy of this publication is also available online at:
http://www.lboro.ac.uk/wedc/publications/

Ghana Project Team Leader: Kwabena Sarpong
Lead Researcher: Dr Kodjo Mensah Abrampah
Small Water Enterprises in Africa 4: Ghana
A study of small water enterprises in Accra

WEDC (The Water, Engineering and Development Centre) at Loughborough University in the UK is one of the world's leading institutions concerned with education, training, research and consultancy for the planning, provision and management of physical infrastructure for development in low- and middleincome countries.

This edition is reprinted and distributed by Practical Action Publishing.
Since 1974, Practical Action Publishing has published and disseminated books and information in support of international development work throughout the world. Practical Action Publishing trades only in support of its parent charity objectives and any profits are covenanted back to Practical Action (Charity Reg. No. 247257, Group VAT Registration No. 880 9924 76).

This document is an output from a project funded by the UK
Department for International Development (DFID)
for the benefit of low-income countries.
The views expressed are not necessarily those of DFID.

Designed at WEDC by Kay Davey
Front cover photo montage by Rod Shaw
Front cover photographs by Cyrus Njiru
Illustrations by Ken Chatterton

Acknowledgements

The editors wish to express gratitude to the in-country study team comprising Kwabena Sarpong Manu (Project Leader and Executive Director, MIME Consult), Dr Kodjo Mensah-Abrampah (Lead Researcher, WaterAid - Dar es Salaam). The editors are also grateful to Paul Kukwaw (Leader of the field survey team, MIME Consult), Ms Aissa Toure (WaterAid Ghana), Stephen Ntow (WaterAid Ghana), Abdul Nasgiru (WaterAid Ghana), and Emmanuel Addai (WaterAid Ghana) for their useful contributions to the report.

The editors wish to thank members of the UK research team comprising Mike Albu (ITDG), Diana Mitlin and Gordon McGranahan for their important role in the research project.

George Acolor and other staff of the Ghana Water Company (GWC) provided useful information and data on the operations of GWC and their perspectives on small water enterprises.

Contents

List of boxes

List of figures

List of photographs

List of tables

Acronyms

AMA	Accra Metropolitan Authority
ATMA	Accra Tema Metropolitan Area (of GWC)
CBD	Central Business District
CBOs	Community-based organizations
CAP	Coalition Against the Privatization of Water
CWSA	Community Water and Sanitation Agency
DFID	Department for International Development
FDB	Food and Drugs Board
GLSS	Ghana Living Standard Survey
GoG	Government of Ghana
GPRS	Ghana Poverty Reduction Strategy
GPRTU	Ghana Private Road Transport Union
GWC	Ghana Water Company
GWSC	Ghana Water and Sewerage Corporation
ITDG	Practical Action (formerly the Intermediate Technology Development Group)
LET	Labour Enterprise Trust
LGAs	Local government authorities
LPZ	Low-pressure zones
MLGRD	Ministry of Local Government and Rural Development
MoWH	Ministry of Works and Housing
NBSSI	National Board for Small-Scale Industries
NDPC	National Development Planning Commission
NGO	Non-governmental organization
PMU	Project Management Unit
PSP	Private sector participation
PURC	Public Utilities Regulatory Commission
PWTOA	Private Water Tanker Owners Association
SSP	Small-scale providers
SWE	Small water enterprises
T&CPD	Town and Country Planning Department
TUC	Trades Union Congress
WEDC	Water, Engineering and Development Centre
WRC	Water Resource Commission

Executive Summary

Introduction

Background

The available data show that some 30 per cent of Ghana's nearly 18.3 million people do not have access to potable water (GoG, 2003). It is also known that many of the remaining 70 per cent depend on informal sources of supply, especially in Accra and other cities. The key operators in this alternative supply 'system' are tanker operators, cart operators, domestic vendors, neighbour-sellers, water-sachet sellers, etc. Despite the significant role played by these groups in urban water delivery, their operations are not appreciated by either the general public or many agencies.

The project 'Better Access to Water in Informal Urban Settlements through Support to Water Providing Enterprises' is a four-country study being undertaken by the Water, Engineering and Development Centre (WEDC) and its local partners in four countries, Ghana, Sudan, Kenya and Tanzania. The Ghana research has been conducted by MIME Consult in collaboration with the in-country research partners, WaterAid and the Ghana Water Company (GWC). Supervisory support was provided by WEDC.

Project goal, purpose and expected output

The project goal is to improve the well-being of poor people in informal urban settlements through cost-effective improved water supply services. The project aims to identify and test constraints, opportunities and strategies for enabling SWEs to deliver acceptable levels of service to poor urban consumers. A key objective of this research is to improve the operating environment for SWEs with a view to improving water services to the urban poor. The final output includes recommendations for undertaking a pilot project in partnership with other stakeholders.

Research methodology and sites

The research methodology involved:

- a desk study/literature review in the areas of: water supply and challenges in serving the urban poor; ongoing reforms in the water sector; public statements and intentions on addressing the water needs of the poor; location of the poor in Accra; operations of small water enterprises;
- the establishment of selection criteria and selection of project communities;
- the design and application of questionnaire/interview/focus discussion guides;
- key informant interviews;
- a survey of small water enterprises (SWEs), and consumer perceptions of the role of SWEs; and
- a stakeholder interface workshop to validate the findings and discuss opportunities for undertaking a pilot project involving a partnership of stakeholders – the utility, an SWE, the community, the regulator, NGOs, and the central and local government authorities.

Two predominantly poor urban communities were selected as the main research communities: **Teshie** and **Ashalley Botwe**.

Findings

Water provision to the urban poor

The issue of water provision to the urban poor is receiving a lot of attention from public agencies – the Ghana Poverty Reduction Strategy (GPRS) Project, the Ministry of Works and Housing, the Public Utilities Regulatory Commission and Ghana's Development Partners. So far, however, this has been more good intentions than actions. It is also clear that many poor people will continue to depend on SWEs for their water supply needs for some time to come, and that private sector participation (PSP) will not in the immediate future outlaw SWEs from the distribution chain.

There are a considerable number of people in Accra who are not served by the Ghana Water Company as a result of a combination of insufficient reticulation, an overall shortage of supply, and an inability to pay the high connection fees, among other things. The statement that water supply coverage in Accra is around 80 per cent hides the problems behind the supply choices available to consumers, particularly the poor, many of whom have to depend on secondary and tertiary providers.

Small water enterprises (SWEs)

Despite of their acknowledged presence in urban water delivery, very little work has been done to understand the role of SWEs, the constraints they face and the impact they make in addressing the needs of the poor. The following summarizes some of the key features of the operations of SWEs.

The SWEs operating in the study communities are:

- tanker operators;
- cart operators;
- domestic vendors;
- neighbour-sellers; and
- water-sachet / ice-block sellers.

All these operators depend on the utility for their primary supplies and form an intermediary supply chain between the utility and the end-user.

Key issues in the operations of SWEs

The key issues concerning the operations of SWEs could be classified as: (a) water supply; (b) finance; (c) water quality; (d) price of water as sold along the SWE supply chain; (e) technology; and (f) recognition of the role and relevance of SWEs. The constraints in these are areas are summarized below:

Supply constraints

- Insufficient filling points and restrictions imposed by the utility on what days and how many hours tankers can operate, result in longer waiting times for tankers, fewer trips, and an inability to meet the supply requirements of vendors and consumers, creating shortages and high end-user prices.
- The lack of alternative supply sources outside the utility limits the scope of SWE operations.

Price constraints

- The tariffs that the GWC charges to tanker associations are higher than the Public Utilities Regulatory Commission (PURC) domestic tariffs. Therefore the full component of tanker prices as sold to vendors comprises (a) higher than domestic (commercial) water tariffs; (b) transportation; and (c) income tax paid by tankers.
- This cost structure translates into higher tanker bulk prices, which in turn results in higher vendor retail prices in the communities. On the other hand, the tankers themselves charge consumers 10-15 per cent above the rates mutually agreed with the utility.

Water quality constraints

- Water quality awareness is generally low.
- Quality assurance procedures along the SWE supply chain are non-existent.
- For vendors, the only means of assessing the quality of tanker supplies is through the colour, odour and taste of the water.
- The PURC is taking a pro-active role in producing guidelines to ensure the quality of water delivered by tankers.

Finance constraints

- Initial investment costs for vehicles and storage facilities are high, credit facilities are unavailable, and these present a huge challenge for their operations.
- Tanker operators rely on very old vehicles (some 20 years old) resulting in high breakdown rates and equally high maintenance costs.

Technology and innovation

- Some means of storage, especially the underground water tanks used by vendors, present a huge challenge to water quality assurance in terms of ease of cleaning and disinfection of tanks. The mechanism of bailing water out of these tanks also increases the risk of contamination. There is a need for innovative interventions in this area.
- The utility has the capacity to look for other sources of water to address local situations and assist SWEs beyond its current traditional sources, and this should be pursued.

Management capacity

SWEs, especially vendors, do not keep proper records and therefore have difficulty assessing their profit margins, especially where they do not separate sales from their own domestic usage.

Recognition

SWEs would like to be given proper recognition so that they can play their roles adequately. It was noted at the workshop, for example, that if SWE operations were properly mainstreamed into the distribution chain, their activities could be regulated and they would have a greater obligation to moderate their charges.

Strategies for addressing constraints

On the basis of the research findings and ideas generated by the stakeholder interface workshop, the following strategies have been proposed for addressing the operational and other constraints of SWEs as identified by this study.

Supply strategies

- The utility / SWEs could develop supplementary supplies from groundwater sources.

Price reduction strategies

- The general tariff design responsibility of the regulator, PURC, must be extended to cover SWE prices.
- Water sales to tanker associations must be priced at the approved domestic rates.
- The utility must install standpipes in low-income communities for direct sales to consumers.
- Community tanks could be installed in low-income communities, so tankers can provide supplies for onward direct retail to consumers, managed by local community-based organizations (CBOs).

Water quality assurance strategies

- The PURC must take responsibility for SWE water quality assurance through periodic disinfection and certification of tankers, using the competencies of agencies like the Ghana Food and Drugs Board, the Ghana Standards Board, and the Ghana Water Company.
- Vendors' storage facilities and general environment must be inspected periodically by town council health inspectors.
- There must be a general education campaign targeting both vendors and the general public on water and health issues through radio, TV, etc.

Finance strategies

- The Government of Ghana (GoG) could consider the possibility of helping organized tanker associations to acquire good vehicles, as they have done for other established transport organizations like the Ghana Private Road Transport Union (GPRTU).
- GoG could consider waiving taxes on imported tanker vehicles.

- Tanker associations must be encouraged to form cooperatives and import inputs like tyres, batteries, etc. for their members.

Strategies for addressing identified technological constraints

- Vendors' reservoirs should be designed to ensure that tap outlets are used instead of bailing the water out with buckets.

Strategies for addressing management capacity constraints

- SWEs should be given training in bookkeeping and basic accounting. The National Board for Small-Scale Industries (NBSSI) expressed a willingness at the workshop to conduct such training.

Strategies for addressing the lack of recognition

- The National Development Planning Commission should examine and capture SWE issues in their policy documents, e.g. the GPRS document.
- The Public Utilities Regulatory Commission must assume some advocacy role for SWEs.
- District assemblies should assume some critical interface with SWEs.

Proposed Phase 2 project activities

Pilot projects

Emanating out of the above research findings and subsequent stakeholder discussions in Dar es Salaam, the Ghanaian team proposes a **community-based bulk water storage pilot scheme**, based on the following strategies:

- Undertake an advocacy process to rescue and recreate the image of SWEs in the eyes of the public. This will involve:
  - Developing platforms for interaction among stakeholders
  - Publishing public outreach materials
  - Holding radio and television discussions on SWEs
  - Arranging fora with policymakers and law-makers on research findings
  - Advocacy for SWEs to serve on water (decision-making) boards and committees
- Provision of bulk water storage points where water from the Ghana Water Company mains could be stored or bulk water from tankers could be discharged for a fee. The community would sign an agreement with a private operator to

manage the facility. The bulk storage source could thus sell water directly to consumers, vendors and motorized cart operators.

- To ensure the quality of the water both vendors and households could be helped to acquire improved storage facilities. The bulk storage will thus ensure a buffer supply being available in addition to that supplied by the tankers. In areas where there are water mains, direct supply from the bulk water sources could be undertaken.

Chapter 1

Background

1.1 Introduction

Available data show that about 30 per cent of Ghana's nearly 18.3 million people have no access to potable water (GoG, 2003). Even many of the 70 per cent who do have access to potable water depend on informal and often irregular sources. Indeed, for reasons of resources, legal status and maintenance, there are many areas and suburbs even within the capital Accra which are under- or unserved by formal suppliers. These areas are served by alternative water supply 'systems', usually water tankers, carts, domestic vendors, neighbour sellers, and water sachet sellers. Most of these areas are known to be occupied by poor people. The providers of these alternative systems are described as small water enterprises (SWEs) or small-scale providers (SSPs).

Regrettably, the services of these providers are not well appreciated by some community members and the agencies that support those communities. In view of the important role these SWEs play, they need to be understood, recognized, and supported to enable their operations to benefit the poor people they serve. The quest to understand this process has resulted in this research, initiated by Water Engineering and Development Centre (WEDC) of the University of Loughborough and working in collaboration with WaterAid Ghana. The research is being conducted in four African cities, namely Harare (Zimbabwe), Dar es Salaam (Tanzania), Khartoum (Sudan) and Accra (Ghana). The Ghanaian study concentrates on the capital city, Accra, and has been carried out by MIME Consult Ltd.

1.2 Project goal

The project goal is to improve the well-being of the poor in informal urban settlements through cost-effective improved water supply services.

1.3 Project purpose and expected outputs

The project aims to identify and test constraints, opportunities and strategies for enabling small water enterprises to deliver an acceptable water service to poor urban consumers. A key objective of this research is to improve the operating environment of SWEs with a view to improving the services they provide. The project plans to identify and pilot practical interventions to improve these services during its second phase.

The expected outputs are as follows:

- Establishment of poor people's demand for water and supply opportunities
- Assessment of the role of SWEs in the water supply system, especially in meeting the water needs of informal poor communities
- An appreciation of the operational issues, constraints and potential of SWEs in serving urban poor people
- An appreciation by the stakeholders of water quality and pricing issues
- Recommendations for undertaking a pilot project in partnership with other stakeholders.

1.4   Purpose and scope of report

This Country Status Report outlines all stages and outputs of Phase 1. The report presents the analyses of the institutional and regulatory arrangements for water supply to poor households (especially by SWEs), findings from the fieldwork on the role and relevance of SWEs, the constraints to their operations, and planning for appropriate interventions.

1.5   Structure of the report

The report is in twelve chapters, as follows:

Chapter 1   provides the background to the study, the project goal and purpose, expected outputs, and purpose of this report.

Chapter 2   covers the water supply situation in the national context.

Chapter 3   examines the water supply in the city of Accra in terms of history, arrangements, infrastructure, legal/regulatory framework and water coverage and demand.

Chapter 4   looks at water demand and poverty. Specific issues discussed include income and expenditure, water usage and access (affordability and water quality), and coping strategies.

Chapter 5   identifies where poor people live, presenting an overview of the types of urban poor settlements in the city of Accra, water supply systems for the poor, and identification of specific locations for the research.

Chapter 6 provides a general overview of SWEs, their operational culture, livelihoods, and role in the water supply chain.

Chapter 7 looks at tanker operations.

Chapter 8 looks at domestic vendors.

Chapter 9 discusses issues on consumer perspectives on SWEs in terms of service options and technology, cost of water, and water quality.

Chapter 10 dwells on the views of utilities and government agencies. Issues discussed include both attitudes and current arrangements to mainstream activities of SWEs into the water-supply chain.

Chapter 11 covers consensus building and opportunities for partnerships, and notes the key issues from the stakeholder workshop.

Chapter 12 defines the proposal for a possible Phase 2 pilot scheme following on from both the findings of the research and the two workshops in Accra and Dar es Salaam.

Chapter 13 highlights the conclusions and recommendations.

1.6 Methodology

Desk study/literature review

A desk study was undertaken, involving a review of existing reports dealing with issues of water supply to urban poor people in Ghana. Specifically, the researchers compiled and reviewed information relating to:

- incidence and trends in poverty in Ghana;
- urban informal communities in Accra;
- the policy dimensions of government, the utility, and regulatory bodies on service delivery to the urban poor and informal settlements; and
- the water supply and accessibility situation and its impact on urban informal communities.

The main secondary data includes information obtained from published documents in the public and private domain, unpublished documents (including seminar papers, etc.), government policy statements, and maps. A list of documents is included in the References and Bibliography, and in Appendix 1.

Interactions with key informants

A list of agencies, individuals and SWEs who met with the research team is presented in Appendix 2. Principal among the institutions were: Ghana Water Company Limited (Accra Tema Metropolitan Area officials), Town and Country Planning Department, the Ghana Poverty Reduction Project/Social Investment

Fund, Public Utilities Regulatory Commission (PURC) and the Project Management Unit (PMU) of the Ministry of Works and Housing, Lashibi Tankers Association, and the Private Water Tanker Owners Association (PWTOA).

Design of information-gathering tools and pre-testing of questionnaires

The tools that were used are consistent with those suggested by the UK Research Team. These included:

- Structured questionnaires – to collect information from (a) tanker operators; (b) cart operators; (c) vendors and neighbour sellers; (d) consumers; and (e) tanker associations.
- Interview guides and checklists – to collect information from identified institutions and key informants.
- Guidelines for Conduct of Focus Group Discussions – to facilitate interaction with groups and to help reach clear conclusions from the discussions.

Samples of these tools are provided in Appendix 3. The Client provided comments on the tools, which were incorporated accordingly. A pre-testing exercise was conducted to assess their appropriateness after which intensive fieldwork began.

The survey covered 28 households, 20 tanker operators and 20 vendors in the localities of Teshie and Ashalley Botwe.

1.7 Studies of SWEs and urban poor communities

A number of studies carried out in the area of service provision to the urban poor provided useful insight into the assignment. A list of these documents and their relevance appears in Appendix 1.

1.8 Definition and context of key terms used in this report

Community

In its theoretical form a community has a more intricate definition, referring to people occupying a common spatial area, sharing a common culture, and having a common organizational relationship and functional co-operation. Relating this to the empirical requirements of this study, 'community' is a defined spatial area with people sharing common facilities and having the potential to co-operate to undertake communal projects. The community as defined in this study is thus guided by the Accra Metropolitan Association's definition of suburbs or electoral areas. The electoral areas have become very effective boundaries for communities as they have become the basis of resource distribution for the Local Government Authority.

Informal settlements

An informal settlement is defined by two key factors, legality and the nature of its growth. The legality or, more mildly, the formality of a settlement is guided by two key statutes: Cap 84 of 1948 and Act 462 of the Local Government Act (1993). These statutes indicate that all settlements must have a site-plan approved by the constituted planning authority (in this case the District Assembly). The site-plan is then gazetted and becomes a legal document, guiding all development activities. It is only when this process has been completed that other agencies and utility providers can install the necessary municipal facilities.

Thus informal settlements in Accra are either very old (Osu, James Town) and predate the legalization of the spatial area, or they developed spontaneously and control activities were usurped (Madina). In many cases such settlements cannot be demolished for obvious social and political reasons, but they may also be precluded by law from obtaining the public facilities they need to support the population.

In Accra there are a number of informal settlements or communities that are located in conflicting land-use areas, or in areas where ownership is contested between clans or individuals. There are many residential developments occupying land allocated to other land uses, and because of this services such as water, electricity, municipal roads and even sanitation facilities have not been formally provided, for example areas around Sowutuom which had been earmarked for an Olympic complex but have been encroached upon.

Urban poor

The urban poor are first defined by income, and in Ghana any adult person who earns less than US$376 is considered poor. By this criterion, only 4 per cent of Accra's population is poor (GSS, 2000a). There are many other significant factors that can be used to define poor, however.[1] The urban poor are generally those receiving less than $376 and who also do not have access to such basic facilities as water, sanitation, health and education. These criteria can usually be detected easily by where the person lives.

Small water enterprises (SWEs)

SWEs refer to enterprises engaged in the provision of water, other than the conventional water utilities. In Ghana, the Ghana Water Company Limited (GWC) is the utility mandated to supply water in the urban areas. All other secondary and tertiary suppliers of water fall within the SWE category. These include water tanker services, motorized cart operators, domestic water vendors (which includes neighbour sellers), water-sachet sellers, and those who deliver water from source to end-user.

---

1. In a recent PURC workshop at which the Project Leader was a participant, the PURC indicated that it was going to adopt a working definition of the urban poor as those:
   - those without access to the utility's supply;
   - who depend on secondary providers; and
   - who purchase water by the bucket.

Chapter 2

Overview of Water Supply in Ghana

2.1 Brief history of water supply in Ghana

At independence in 1957, Ghana had about 35 pipe-borne water systems. In 1958, the Water Supply Division, under the Ministry of Works and Housing, was created to be responsible for both urban and rural water supply. The division was transformed into the Ghana Water and Sewerage Corporation (GWSC) by an act of parliament in 1966, with an added responsibility of establishing and operating sewerage services. The act charged the corporation to 'provide and manage potable water supply and sewerage services for domestic and industrial purposes throughout the country'. By the early 1990s, GWSC was operating some 208 pipe-borne systems and over 1,000 point sources all over the country.

2.2 Management of water supply systems

There are two very distinct water supply arrangements in Ghana. These are:

- **Urban water supply** involves the provision of water services (mainly drinking water supply) through generally complex water distribution systems serving large urban centres of population (usually exceeding 50,000). Urban water supply is managed by the Ghana Water Company. Tariffs for urban water supply are regulated through the Public Utilities Regulatory Commission.
- **Community water supply** involves the provision of water supply through point sources (wells and boreholes) and small pipe-borne systems servicing rural and small town communities. Communities, through their water management boards, set their own tariffs, which are then approved by their respective District Assembly. Since 1994 a demand-driven approach, with public sector facilitation and support, has been the key principle for development of the rural and small town water supply. Communities contribute 5 per cent to the capital cost of projects.

The Ministry of Works and Housing (MoWH), which has responsibility for water, notes that urban and community water supplies would be differentiated on the basis of their funding and management arrangements, with urban systems being managed (in principle) on a commercial basis to achieve full cost recovery. Rural and small town water supply will continue, in the near future, to have their capital costs subsidized whilst communities meet their operation and maintenance and some replacement costs (MoWH, 2004).

2.3   Current water supply situation

Despite efforts to increase access to potable water supply, the gap between demand and supply has continued to widen. It is projected that the demand for water will increase to 246 million cubic metres by 2005 and 432 million cubic metres by 2025, compared to the current supply of 166 million cubic metres. The 2000 Population Census statistics show that in Ghana 42.1 per cent of households have access to pipe-borne water either directly or through a tanker service, while a third (33 per cent) use a well or borehole. The remaining 25 per cent of households depend on natural water sources such as rainwater, rivers and ponds (GoG, 2000b).

2.4   Urban water coverage

GWC currently operates 86 urban water supply systems throughout the country, with a total installed capacity of about 737,000 m³/day. Present urban potable water demand is estimated at 995,000 m³/day, whilst supply is 551,451 m³/day. Figure 2.1 gives a picture of national urban water coverage, with an average of 59 per cent of people covered (GWC figures).

2.5   Urban water sector challenges

MoWH has identified a number of challenges facing the urban water sector. Based on these it is now reviewing its policies and programmes to address the current shortfalls (MoWH, 2004). These challenges include:

- A need for improved management in operations and maintenance of water supply.
- Service quality and coverage are low, and tariffs are not linked to level of service.
- Difficulty in setting tariffs to achieve cost recovery in view of the high level of wastage (high levels of unaccounted-for water, estimated at 52 per cent).
- Inadequate revenue and investment, in large part the result of excessively old facilities.
- Mechanisms to ensure accessibility to potable water supply by low-income and peri-urban consumers are inadequate.

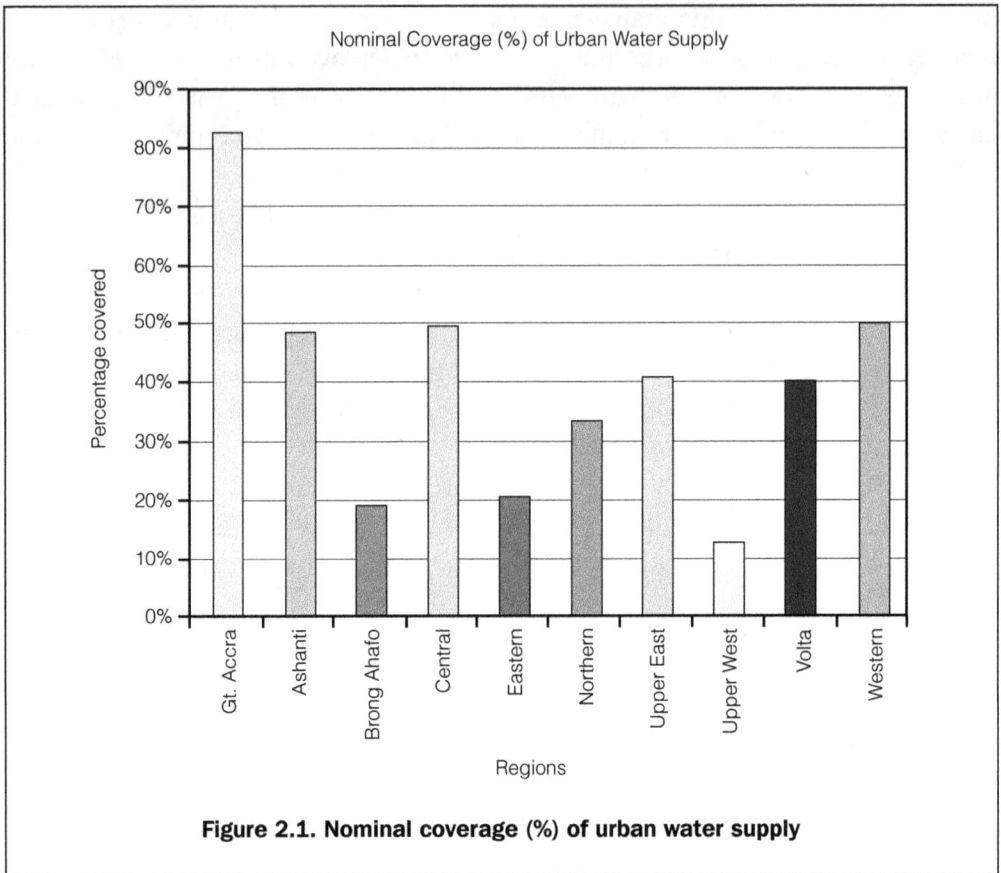

Figure 2.1. Nominal coverage (%) of urban water supply

Since 1998 GWC has transferred over 110 small town systems to District Assemblies for community management, and this has reduced the strain that was being put on the utility by these (mostly subsidized) systems.

2.6 Key institutions in the water sector

The key institutions in the urban water sector, whose remits have a bearing on the provision of water and, in particular, service to low-income/poor communities, are:

- Ministry of Works and Housing
- Ghana Water Company
- Project Management Unit/Water Sector Restructuring Secretariat
- Public Utilities Regulatory Commission
- Ghana Poverty Reduction Strategy Project (National Development Planning Commission)
- Local Government Authority
- NGO and CBOs

The issue of the extent to which current policies and strategies support pro-poor water provision, the regulation and monitoring of the activities of SWEs, and the perceived impact on low-income households are discussed in Chapter 10. A matrix of the roles and responsibilities of various institutions appears in Appendix 4. A few are discussed below.

Ministry of Works and Housing (MoWH)

The MoWH is responsible for setting the water policies for the country – both resource management and the supply of drinking water (both urban and rural). These policies are carried out through its various agencies, such as the Department of Hydrology, the Public Works Department, and the Water Sector. The focus of the MoWH for the past few years has been on creating a framework for improved efficiency and accelerated investments in the water sector to meet the goals enshrined in the Ghana Poverty Reduction Strategy (GPRS). A process to introduce private sector participation (PSP) in urban water supply has been inordinately delayed, aggravating an already bad water supply situation. The process is being managed by the Project Management Unit (PMU), which also has responsibility for the investment programme associated with the reforms.

Ghana Water Company (GWC)

GWC is the only utility responsible for the provision of drinking water in Ghana's urban areas and some small towns. It has regional offices in all 10 regions of Ghana, each headed by a Regional (Chief) Manager. The utility notes that its services are informed by pro-poor considerations, as in the use of standpipes in certain communities and in the application of lifeline tariffs. In addition, the utility has a policy not to discriminate between communities when planning piped reticulation systems.[2] The utility is pro-poor, and tries to treat all communities equally, regardless of wealth.

Public Utilities Regulatory Commission (PURC)

The Public Utilities Regulatory Commission (PURC) is an independent body established in 1997 to oversee the financial regulation of public utilities (water and electricity). The key functions of the PURC include (a) providing guidelines on, and the examination and approval of rates chargeable for, the provision of utility services; (b) protecting the interests of both consumers and providers of utility services; (c) promoting fair competition among public utilities; (d) initiating and conducting investigations into the quality standards of customer services; and (e) monitoring performance standards of service provision. Since its establishment the PURC has been responsible for regulating the operations of GWC and developing guidelines and standards of performance. The Commission is currently developing a pro-poor agenda to address service provision to the urban poor.

Water Resources Commission (WRC)

The Water Resources Commission (WRC) is responsible for regulating and managing the use of water resources, and for the co-ordination of any policy related to its functions. WRC's remit is particularly relevant to the activities of SWEs if one considers the emerging evidence that some SWEs who are taking water from source (mostly boreholes) to end-user need to be regulated, particularly in relation to their water abstraction activities.

Town and Country Planning Department (T&CPD)

Under the Local Government Act of 1993 the Town and Country Planning Department (T&CPD) is the Local Government Authority technical institution that approves and controls all infrastructure development. The amendment (Cap 84) to the Town and Country Planning Ordinance of 1945, requires strict guidelines and processes for the development of reticulation systems and even the legality of the undertaking. The inadequacies in T&CPD's operations have impinged on the provision of services for a number reasons: (a) large settlements have developed in a number of areas in the cities which had been earmarked for other purposes; (b) a number of buildings are not adequately covered by appropriate authorizations; and (c) utilities have been overstretched trying to cope with the spate of unauthorized developments.

In recent years the utilities have not sought planning approval from T&CPD before connecting potential customers to the mains. This is because it is widely accepted that the department's inability to keep up with developments should not hold back the pace of new service provision.[3]

Local Government Authority (LGA)

In line with Ghana's decentralization programme, Local Government Authorities (LGAs) – Metropolitan, Municipal, and District Assemblies – have been given clear-cut quasi-legislative and administrative powers enshrined in the Local Government Act 462 of 1993. The Ministry of Local Government and Rural Development (MLGRD) has in recent years received donor support for a number of urban renewal projects [Urban I-VI] in which water and sanitation have been key components. The Ministry considers these projects as pro-poor because they seek to improve the living conditions of the urban poor and low-income households. LGAs have a number of sub-structures, including Urban Councils (Sub-metro councils) and Unit Committees. Unit Committees form the base structure of the local administration system and their specific objectives are to be in close contact with the people on matters concerning education, organization of communal labour, revenue raising, environmental cleanliness, etc. As such, the input of

Assembly and Unit Committee members into both sensitizing and organizing the community and developing arrangements to serve the poor in deprived areas cannot be overlooked.

Local government structures have not yet considered the operations of SWEs as a relevant aspect of community development. Indeed LGAs covered by the urban water systems have played little or no role at all in water delivery to support GWC. No specific guidelines exist on location of vending points, water quality, or health inspections.

NGOs and CBOs

There is a significant presence of non-government organizations (NGOs) in rural and community water supply, where it is estimated that they contribute around 8.25 per cent of the ongoing developments (PPIAF/CWSA, 2002). Their activities have not been seen in the cities and major urban areas in relation to water supply interventions, however. WaterAid, which has worked mainly on community water supply projects in Ghana, now seeks to bring their experience in dealing with the urban poor in other parts of the world (and also to learn from others) in undertaking pro-poor urban water supply interventions. On the other hand, civil society groups such as the Integrated Social Development Centre (ISODEC) and the Trades Union Congress have been very vocal in their opposition to the planned private sector participation in urban water supply, citing marginalization of the poor as their major concern.

However, community-based organizations have been quite active in creating access to pipe-borne water in urban areas, particularly in the new residential suburbs of Accra. Some CBOs and residents' associations fund mains extensions to their communities, such as the West Legon Residents' Association and Adenta Residents' Association. They raise funds to buy the pipes whilst the pipe-laying is done either directly by the utility or under their supervision. The associations charge prospective customers or new entrants into the community who wish to connect to 'their' mains. By this arrangement, they are able to recoup some or all of the original investment. An examination of the list of such residents associations reveals that they are mostly middle to upper-income people who are able to afford the initial contributions (MIME, 2002; GWC). This practice helps to expand coverage, but it is also one that obviously excludes the poor from accessing direct house connections,[4] particularly in peri-urban and economically mixed areas.

Urban water sector reforms

Reforms in the urban water sector have sought to address the nagging problems of inadequate supply, high rates of unaccounted-for-water, inability to recover costs due to low tariffs, and weaknesses in management. The policy objectives have been defined by the Ministry of Works and Housing as being to (a) address availability and accessibility; (b) improve sector management through private sector participation; and (c) achieve financial equilibrium through cost recovery, whilst addressing the interests of the poor.

A major challenge with PSP is the need to balance the commercial and social goals of water supply and ensure that the poor and vulnerable will have access to an appropriate, affordable service. Mechanisms to ensure that the vulnerable are catered for are vital, and some of these are being defined in the contract documents. Studies such as 'Ghana Urban Water Supply: Demand assessment and willingness to pay' (London Economics, 1999), 'Social Mapping of Some Poor Communities' (ISODEC, 1999), and 'Promoting the Development of Arrangements to Serve the Urban Poor' (MIME Consult, 2002) have been conducted as part of the processes. The MoWH is to set up a unit that will focus on the needs of the poor and the vulnerable (Manu, 2001). A social connection fund is also being considered to help poor people to connect.

Discussions with the reform secretariat indicate that SWEs will continue to play a significant role in water supply for some time to come. The principal reasons are:

- There is such a huge gap in meeting investment requirements that not all communities can be served in the near future.[5]
- Because of poor planning in some cities (for example Nima, Sukura and some parts of Teshie in Accra), the utility would need to work with SWEs to be able to reach some areas in a cost-effective manner.
- The relatively high incidence of urban poverty and both poor people's inability to make house connections or their preference for other supply and payment options makes delivery through SWEs a preferred choice.

No attempts have been made to exclude tanker operations from PSP. Indeed, under the envisaged contracts, provision will be made for SWEs, especially tanker services, and for a certain amount of water to be given to these SWEs to ensure fairness and equity.[6] Similarly, there is a policy to re-introduce standpipes in some poor communities in Accra and other major cities, where these had previously been discontinued. Given its experience in the past, GWC prefers to deal with individual private vendors, who can be held accountable for the water that is sold.[7]

Recap of institutional roles and relevance to SWEs

The available evidence is that only GWC has a formal relationship with SWEs. This is through bilateral agreements with, for example, the tanker associations. Through the agreements with the tanker associations, GWC attempts to loosely regulate their operations in the areas of water quality and price. Indeed, depending on which organization you talk to, SWEs are seen as exploiters or at best a nuisance to other water consumers, because it is perceived that their activities deprive some people from getting a reliable piped water supply. At the Launch Workshop for the project held in 2002, it was quite clear that many people perceived SWEs as exploiters whose activities ought to be curtailed or controlled.

Neither the PURC nor any government body has in the past specifically regulated or supported the operations of SWEs. The MoWH and the PURC are now increasingly recognizing the role that SWEs have been playing and are addressing ways in which they can be made more useful.

The T&CPD, in their design and planning of urban areas, has never considered the case of SWEs nor the provision of utility services to informal communities. The plan always assumes a piped distribution system to be provided by the public utility. For the T&CPD, the informal communities do not 'exist', as no formal provision is made for them for facilities and services. These attitudes and perceptions are changing, however, and either through silent acquiescence or through active encouragement by the public, informal settlements are getting serviced by either the utility or SWEs.

---

2. This came out during discussions with the ATMA Chief Manager (Accra East) – 28th April 2004.

3. From discussions between Lead Researcher and Deputy Director of T&CPD, January 2004.

4. For a new connection, a customer makes two separate payments, the sum of which is higher than the cost of a direct connection to the utility's own mains (where this option exists). These payments are:
   * fees to the CBO, after which permission is granted for connection; and
   * the Ghana Water Company Limited new service connection fees.
   Poor people who reside in these areas are unable to make these payments and therefore cannot get connected.

5. According to the Project Management Unit for the Urban Water Sector Restructuring Project, the urban water sector requires a total investment of some US$1 billion over the next decade to bring total coverage to 85 per cent. So far the amount committed through the World Bank and other donors is US$150 million under the proposed five-year management contract.

6. These were provided for under the Draft Lease Contracts prepared in 1999/2000. Even though there has been a change to a management contract, there is no reason to believe that the pro-poor clauses will disappear in the new draft contracts.

7. Discussions with all three Regional Directors in Greater Accra revealed their preference for dealing with commissioned vendors, as the utility does not have the expertise to sell water at that level (through standpipes), and their experience in dealing with community organizations has not been good.

Chapter 3

Water Supply Situation in Accra

3.1 Water infrastructure

Greater Accra is served by two water treatment plants – Kpong Treatment Plant, which supplies the eastern corridor of the city, and Weija Treatment Plant, which supplies the western sections of Accra. The two systems have a total capacity of 350,000 m³ per day, whilst demand is estimated at 430,000 m³.

Kpong Water System

The Kpong Treatment Works treats water from the Volta River some 54 km away and pumps it to Accra. The raw water is drawn from the Volta at an intake approximately 17 km downstream from the Akosombo Dam and the Works consists of two parts: the old treatment plant supplying rural areas, and the new plant supplying urban areas. Their respective capacities are 30,000 m³/day (7 mgd) and 160,000 m³/day (35 mgd). For urban areas, the treated water is pumped to the industrial city of Tema from the High-Lift pumping station, which has a maximum output of about 172,800 m³/day 38 mgd). From Tema water is pumped again, to Accra East. Water from the Accra terminal reservoir is transmitted either by gravity or pumped to different pressure zones in Accra. Originally meant to supply a population of some 500,000, this plant has not seen any major expansion in production despite the near tripling of the population of Accra East and Tema City – the two major areas it serves. Kpong's major cost is in energy use as it has to pump treated water several kilometres before it reaches Accra.

Weija Water System

The Weija Treatment Plant is located 15 km west of Accra. The raw water is drawn from the Densu River, which is impounded by the Weija Dam. From the intake, the water is pumped to the treatment works via two pumping stations: the Old Weija Pumping Station and the New Weija Pumping Station. The treatment plant is located 800 m from the dam, on a hill at an elevation of about 100 m, and is composed of four plants. The water is transmitted by gravity to Accra and the various villages on the western side of the city. The Densu Basin has seen a lot of pollution in recent years and this has affected raw water quality in the Weija Dam. GWC therefore spends substantial amounts on chemicals to treat water from Weija.

3.2   Water distribution in Accra

The Accra Tema Metropolitan Area (ATMA) water supply system is currently managed through three regional offices, each headed by a Chief Manager. This is the case because the supply area is large and provides more than 60 per cent of the company's revenues. The three regions are: Tema, Accra East and Accra West. Both Tema and Accra East depend on the Kpong Water Supply system whilst Accra West depends on the Weija Water System.

Accra West

Water to consumers is distributed using three pressure zones based on the general elevation of the Accra supply area. These are the High, Medium and Low Pressure Zones. The Low Pressure Zone (LPZ) covers the lowest areas of Accra in the west, south and east and part of the north of the city. It is the largest supply area of Accra and has, within its boundaries, the main commercial centre, the main administrative centres, an industrial area, and some of the largest residential areas. The Weija Water System supplies water to nearly all the LPZs of the reticulated areas of Accra through its six transmission lines. These areas include Kasoa, Dansoman, Gbawe, Anyaa, Kaneshie, Achimota, Korle Bu, Industrial Area and Accra Central (Oguah, 2004).

Tema and Accra East

Production from Kpong serves Tema Region and eastern parts of Accra. Tema has extensive rural fringes that are served as well. The areas covered under the Tema region have relatively stable 24-hour supply except when efforts are made to supply Teshie, which is a low-income high pressure zone in the eastern part of Accra. The Region also supplies the water needs of heavy industrial and commercial concerns.

Accra East also covers extensive areas of Accra and is evidently among the most deprived of the regions in Accra in terms of water supply. Significant deprived areas (in terms of water coverage) include: Teshie, Adenta, Ashongman, Hatso, Domi, East Legon, Kotobabi, parts of Mamobi, Nima, Newtown and all the areas north of Tetteh Quarshie Circle (Ashalley Botwe, Pantang). The customers include households as well as industries and commercial consumers. Accra East covers most of the middle to high-income areas (including East Legon, North Legon, West Legon), a number of educational institutions, an industrial area (including those producing beverages such as Coca Cola), Labone, Airport Residential Area, Teshie Nungua Estates, etc.

3.3 Water rationing in Accra

One significant fact is that whereas coverage for Accra Tema Metropolitan Area (from the numbers given by GWC) appears to be very high (82 per cent), the evidence is that many poor communities rely on secondary and tertiary suppliers (BiG/ASI, 2002). Groundwater sources are largely saline and unsuitable for drinking or using for a number of other activities (WRI). Thus unlike in other regional centres few poor people depend on wells and boreholes as secondary sources of supply. This means an increasing reliance on SWEs who sell water produced by the utility.

> *"We have had to resort to water rationing in order to meet the needs of more people in our supply area"*

ATMA (East) Chief Manager

GWC currently rations water in most areas of Accra city, especially in areas on the eastern supply network, with some areas getting supply only one or two days a week. Others receive no water for weeks at a time. Table 3.1 below shows a typical daily ration report for the Accra North-East District (Madina, a largely low-income suburb).

Table 3.1. Sample Supply Situation Report					
29/12/2003, Accra North-East District					
Area	Supply duration		Flow situation		Remarks
	Previous	Present	Previous	Present	
North-Legon, Agbogba	6 hrs	8hrs	Poor	Fair	
Kotwi Krom	2hrs	3hrs	Poor	Poor	Flow could not reach most parts of the area
New Road	6hrs	8hrs	Fair	Fair	
Rawlings Circle, Asanka Local	No flow	3hrs	No flow	Poor	Faulty valve hindered flow
Madina Estate (Top)	No flow	No flow	No flow	No flow	
Madina Down	No flow	No flow	No flow	No flow	

Rationing of water is carried out in such a way that if an area misses its turn, as a result of a power outage, for example, then residents have to find other water sources until it is their turn again. To cope with rationing many households have spent substantial sums of money building storage capacity – overhead and underground tanks – to collect sufficient water for the coming week and beyond. One consumer in Northern Teshie, whose area is on a weekly ration, indicated that he has not had to purchase water from tankers for several months because he has sufficient storage for three weeks' supply. Therefore if the area should miss its turn in the ration schedule for up to two weeks, he would still have water in his tank.

Poor respondents in Southern Teshie could not afford to buy storage tanks. The cheapest tank costs ¢1.2 million for an 800-litre tank, which stores enough water for six days for a household of five. It should also be appreciated, however, that given the living conditions, the space requirements would hinder people from installing larger storage tanks.

Major problems in water delivery

The major problems facing the Accra Tema Metropolitan Area – from the perspective of the utility and as gathered during our interaction with key officials of the utility – can be summarized as follows:

- Intermittent supply as a result of water production from Weija and Kpong falling short of demand in the supply areas. This also stems from insufficient pressure during peak hours, power outages, and planned maintenance shutdowns (Regional Engineer, Accra West).
- The high cost of treating raw water as a result of algae formation in dams, and more importantly pollution of the Densu Basin.
- An inadequate distribution network, as a result of which consumers have to lay long pipelines to connect to service lines, with implications for water quality.
- Pipelines, fittings, and specials (non-standard fittings) are all old. Some of the pipework was done in the 1930s when the Weija was first commissioned. This results in frequent leaks and bursts; 10 to 20 leaks and bursts in the supply area are reported and repaired each day.

---

8.   It should be noted that because most properties in Ghana are generally owner-developed and financed, rather than purchased through estate developers or with mortgages, it takes a long time for houses to be completed.

Chapter 4

Locating the Poor in Accra

4.1 City of Accra: Planning and development of Accra

The Greater Accra Metropolitan Area comprises Accra Metropolitan Area, parts of Tema Municipal District, and the Ga District. Accra is Ghana's political and administrative capital, being both the seat of government and Ghana's major commercial centre. Figure 4.1 shows a map of Central Accra. The city and its administrative areas are managed by the Accra Metropolitan Assembly in accordance with the Local Government Act, 1993 (Act 462). The structure of the assembly includes sub-metros, town councils, and unit committee areas.

The development of Accra is based on statutory planning zones to which major land uses have been assigned. The land pattern – as set down mainly by the Town and Country Planning Department – is required to ensure consistent development of the city. During the last thirty years the increasing demand for housing resulting from the large inflow of people from other regions has culminated in uncontrolled development, where the development of residential housing has been far ahead of statutory planning. Given this situation several suburbs have sprung up within the city, resulting in conflicting land uses. Some of these are informal and thus the provision of utilities constitutes a serious problem to the government and utility providers.

4.2 Demography

Accra is Ghana's largest city, with a population more than twice the size of the second city, Kumasi. The 2000 population census (see Table 4.1) puts the population of Greater Accra Region at 2,905,726 (87.7 per cent urban) and the population of Accra metropolis at 1,658,937 (100 per cent urban population), with an estimated 4.5 per cent growth per annum. Approximately 14 per cent of the total population of Ghana (approximately 21 million) live in the Greater Accra Region.

The census information reveals that Accra has its fair share of Ghana's poor, with 26 per cent of the population being classified as 'poor' because they receive less than 66 per cent of the national per capita income. 3.7 per cent of the population are classified as 'hard-core poor' as they earn less than 25 per cent of the national per capita income (see Table 4.2). In 2000, the World Bank estimated that the gross national income per capita for Ghana was US$1900 (Globalis, undated).

Accra settlement patterns include the affluent, middle class, and poor. Recent trends in settlement patterns include the increasing intrusion of middle and upper-income households into peri-urban areas as the city has expanded, which has resulted in mixed communities of rich and poor (T&CPD). This has had the effect of increasing pressure on utilities to provide services to these areas, which requires different supply options. The increasing intrusion of middle and upper-income households into peri-urban areas has had both positive and negative effects, as summarized in Box 4.1.

Table 4.1. Population data for Accra

Total population	Sex	
	Male	Female
1,658,937	817,373	841,564
	49.3%	50.7%

Source: GoG, 2003.

Table 4.2. Population poverty characteristics of Accra

Poverty levels by income		
Non-poor	1,182,822	71.3%
Poor (including hard-core poor) (<66% of national income)	431,323	26.0%
Hard-core poor (the poorest of the poor) (<25% of national income)	61,380	3.7%
Note: Figures and percentages in Table 4.2 are approximate.		

Source: GoG, 2003.

Box 4.1. Impacts of peri-urban growth

Some of the positive and negative effects of recent trends in peri-urban growth include:

- The formation of community-based organizations (CBOs) in peri-urban areas, made up of households who are willing to pay to extend the distribution network, means that those who are unable to pay (the poor living in these communities) may not be served or connected to the system.
- Increasing numbers of poor people are being displaced further out into peri-urban areas, thus making utilities less and less accessible to them.
- The provision of water supply services may not be suited or targeted to poor households.
- Improvements in planning prevent squatters or slum-creating practices from flourishing, and are creating easier access to low-income dwelling units. Evidence of this can be found in East Legon (Shiashie), Madina (Zongo), and Ashalley Botwe (North), all suburbs of Accra.

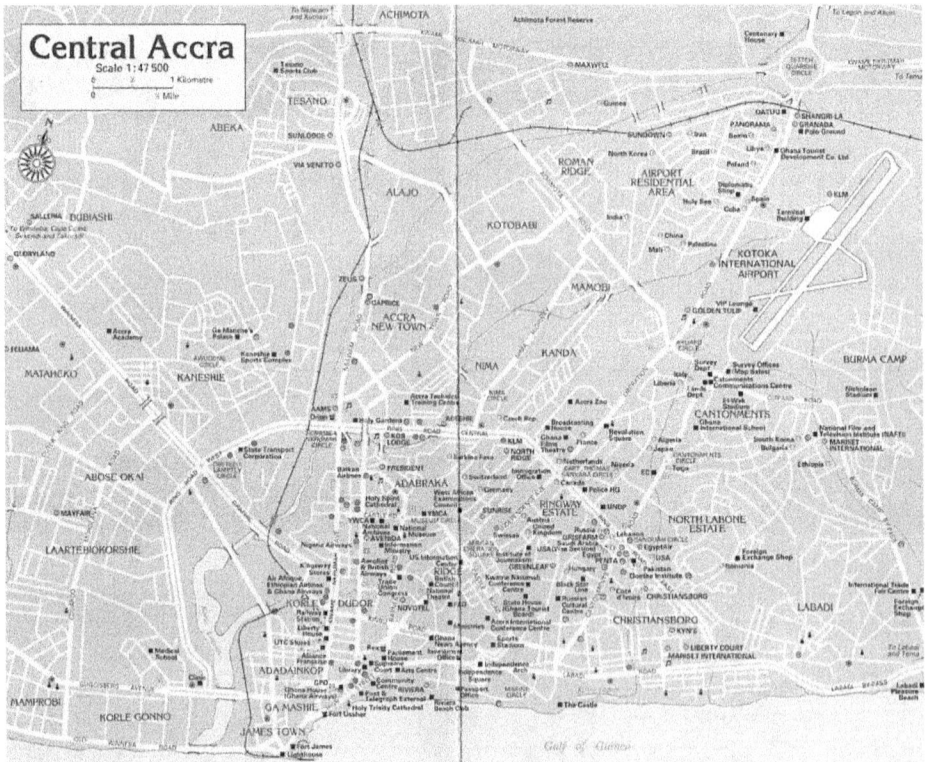

Figure 4.1. Map of Central Accra, showing various suburbs

Source: Macalester, Undated.

4.3   Criteria for selection of study sites

Sixteen informal settlements were considered for selection, using a number of criteria. The following is a summary of the principal criteria used to choose the sites:

- Legality of settlement
- Water service – reliably served, served but irregular (not reliable) and underserved
- Age and morphology of the community – newly developing sites with ongoing intense construction and old settlements with low-quality physical structures
- Economic characteristics – low-income communities
- Social characteristics – indigenous Ga Communities, mixed ethnic (cosmopolitan) communities.

4.4   Selected study areas

Given the study requirements and the purposive criteria used, Teshie and Ashalley Botwe were selected for the study, because:

- Teshie is an informal indigenous settlement with low income levels in the core settlement and it is underserved with water.
- Ashalley Botwe is an informal, mixed-group settlement, with low income levels in the core and it is underserved/unserved with water.

Teshie is a mixed community with a large indigenous population, mainly from the Ga group. It is generally a low-income community and is situated on the coast between Accra and Tema. Most of Teshie is off the water reticulation system, whilst areas with reticulation do not receive water regularly because of the pressure required. Most Teshie residents therefore depend on tankers, cart operators, and

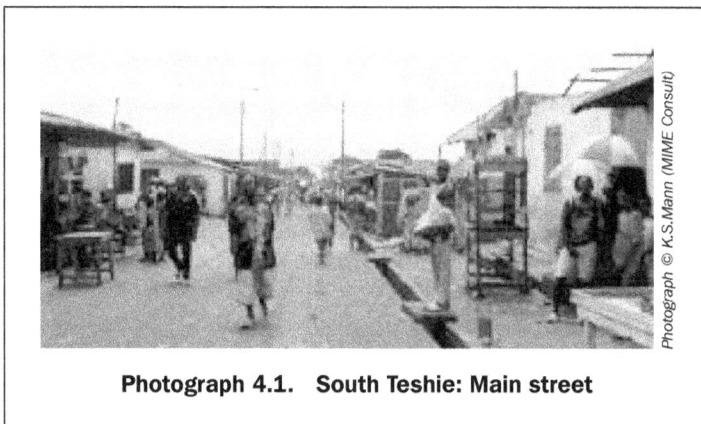

Photograph 4.1.   South Teshie: Main street

Photograph © K.S.Mann (MIME Consult)

vendors for much of their water supply. The indigenous inhabitants of Teshie have lately been very vocal about their water supply situation and have taken a 'no water no vote' stand if nothing is done.

South Teshie is the coastal part of the community and is inhabited mostly by the Gas, who traditionally are fishermen and fish processors. The southern part, which is the old town, has fewer people but a higher population density (see Table 4.3). Although there are water mains in this part of the settlement, water has not flowed there for the past three years. While the utility claims that the pipes are very old and have to be changed, the residents allege that the lack of supply is deliberate so that the high-income areas in adjoining communities could be served. More importantly, the utility argues that because the areas of lower elevation are inhabited by relatively more affluent people, the residents have installed large storage tanks which have to be filled before the water is able to flow to the higher elevation areas. Therefore when pressures are low during a particular ration day in the week, the tanks take a long time to fill and the poorer inhabitants do not receive water. This state of affairs can be repeated for several weeks.

Table 4.3. Demographic information on South Teshie

Population	Sex		No. of houses	Average no. of people per house	No. of households (families)	Average household (family) size
	Male	Female				
35,410	16,529	17,273	2,226	16	8,025	4.4
	46.7%	53.3%				

Source: National Census, 2002.

Table 4.4. Demographic information on North Teshie

Population	Sex		No. of houses	Average no. of people per house	No. of households (families)	Average household (family) size
	Male	Female				
56,949	27,815	29,134	4,862	11.6	12,707	4.5
	48.8%	48.8%				

Source: National Census, 2002.

North Teshie has a mixed population, though the traditional Gas still dominate. At North Teshie, there are relatively newer houses and the population is not as dense as in South Teshie, as shown by the lower population per house ratio in Table 4.4. Water flows at least once every two weeks, according to the residents, but much of the area is not served at all and is mostly occupied by relatively poorer people.

Ashalley Botwe is also an informal community. It is a newly developing community with many uncompleted sites and temporary structures. It is a multi-ethnic community with generally low-income households and a few well-to-do people. There is no reticulation system as the utility's mains are about 3 km away and the community may continue to depend on tankers and vendors for quite some time. It is described as a 'moving community', in the sense that many of the houses have yet to be completed and their owners have therefore not moved in.[8] The poor who are currently living in these houses are there as temporary occupants, in part to protect the property. These poor occupants have in many cases been able to secure unauthorized lands – often land allocated for public land use – and have put up their 'own' structures. Table 4.5 shows basic demographic data for Ashalley Botwe.

As long as the water mains continue to be 3 km away, with insufficient water to go round, the services of the SWEs will be very crucial here. As the rich move in the poor will also move further out, forming new communities, and the services of the SWEs will trail them. It is worth noting that as long as housing development is happening faster than mains are being laid, SWEs will continue to serve this moving population of the poor in peripheral Accra.

Table 4.5.	Demographic information on Ashalley Botwe					
Population	Sex		No. of houses	Average no. of people per house	No. of households (families)	Average household (family) size
	Male	Female				
11,974	6037	5937	1,667	7.2	2,414	5.0
	50.4%	49.6%				

Source: National Census, 2002.

After selecting the two sites, Table 4.6 was applied to capture the variations, if any, and the specific adaptations.

Table 4.6. Comparison between Teshie and Ashalley Botwe			
Community	**Source of water**	**Income status**	**State of service**
Teshie	Tankers Carts Vendors Neighbour sellers	Low	Permanent
Ashalley Botwe	Tankers Carts Vendors	Low Middle	Moving community

Source: Fieldwork

---

8.   It should be noted that because most properties in Ghana are generally owner-developed and financed, rather than purchased through estate developers or with mortgages, it takes a long time for houses to be completed.

Chapter 5

Water Demand and Poverty

5.1 Introduction

The objective of this chapter is to establish an understanding about the poor in Accra and their water needs. The chapter discusses the characteristics of the poor, their water supply needs, access and usage, and their coping strategies. It is largely based on findings from the survey work and literature of earlier work by others.

5.2 Characteristics of poor people

Poverty has many dimensions and assessment depends on a range of indicators. In Ghana, however, the standard measurement of poverty by both incidence and levels is income. On this basis it was asserted in 1998 that any adult who received less than ¢900,000 per annum was 'poor', and less than ¢700,000 was 'hardcore poor'. The corresponding figure for 2004 has not been assessed, but any person who received less than about two-thirds of GDP per capita is considered poor. Ghana's GDP per capita was about US$420 (¢3.7 million) in 2004, so the inferred poverty line from the Ghana Poverty Reduction Strategy Report is $280 (¢2.5million) (GoG, 2003).

According to the Ghana Poverty Reduction Strategy Report, 54 per cent of rural communities in Ghana are poor, while the general urban figure is 27 per cent. In the same report 26 per cent of the residents of Accra metropolis were poor (GoG, 2003). Given the population of Accra, it means that 431,323 people are poor, compared to the total of 6,900,000 nationwide. This means that Accra metropolis has 3.7 per cent of the total poor (GSS, 2000a). Accra metropolis thus presents the highest concentration of the poor with 431,323 statistically identified as being poor (GSS, 2000a). The concentration of the poor in particular communities within Accra and the total absence of social safety nets makes their case even more precarious.

It has been established by Mensah-Abrampah (1999) and Kunfaa (2000) that the urban poor are more vulnerable than the rural poor because in rural areas there are established networks or coping strategies and safety-nets available, while this is not the case in urban communities. Although the competitive nature of the urban setup within a complex economic system creates opportunities, poor people cannot easily access these.

Poor people in Accra can generally be divided into three groups: (a) the indigenous poor; (b) the newly arrived opportunity seekers, and (c) those without reliable livelihoods. The indigenous poor are mostly the traditional Gas whose key livelihood sources have been displaced because of urbanization. The traditional inhabitants of Accra were mostly fishermen, living on a part of the coast stretching from Dansoman to Teshie.

Accra has a population density of 895 per km^2 compared to a national average of 79 per km^2 (GSS, 2000b). Therefore in addition to their economic deprivation, the indigenous poor live in very densely populated areas, deprived of practically any social facilities and any opportunity to get out of the poverty trap. Many people living in communities along the coast of Accra fall into this category.

The **newly arrived** opportunity seekers are also referred to as the **transitional poor**. They are mostly young people who have arrived in Accra from the rural areas 'seeking greener pastures'. They arrive without skills, without any reliable resources, and worst of all with nowhere to live in Accra. They usually end up in areas around the Central Business District (CBD) of Accra, or settle in informal areas where rents are relatively cheaper. Many of these people are single and engage in menial and irregular jobs.

The third group is in fact a result of the two earlier groups. This group is the **poor who do not have any reliable source of livelihood**. A lot of these people were once able workers who have no regular employment or are too old to work. This group, as a result of their age, cannot undertake menial jobs, thus making their situation even worse. Many of them do not even have the means to access social services, including water. Many of these people live in informal settlements, in some cases in old discarded homes owned by family members.

5.3 Poor people's homes

The poor may live anywhere in Accra, even in very high-income areas. This underlines the very mixed nature of Ghanaian society. There are, however, numerous settled communities of relatively poor individuals and households.

The poor are located in three key areas: (a) along the beach (mostly indigenous people); (b) mixed in with the commercial activities at the CBD; and finally (c) in the newly developing peripheral areas. While those on the coastal areas live in old family houses, some over 100 years old, those around the CBD are in make-shift structures, kiosks, and discarded metal containers. At the periphery the poor survive in uncompleted structures and act as caretakers for the new buildings. As the buildings are completed and the high-income owners take charge, the poor will move on to new areas under construction. Often some of them are employed by the new owners as home helps or watchmen.

5.4 Water supply accessibility

Water supply accessibility in Ghana is dependent on whether there is reticulation, available supply, and how affordable it is to connect to the piped system. A socio-economic survey undertaken on behalf of the Public Utilities Regulatory Commission (PURC) showed that connection fees are indeed a barrier to access

---

Box 5.1. Some factors inhibiting slum development in Accra

The continuous development of slums in Accra appears to be reversing. There are two major reasons for this.

The first is a long-term strategy initiated by individual poor households and families to send a family member abroad. A family property may thus be sold off in exchange for a visa and ticket to Europe, America or Japan. Many poor family members were sent abroad and three key results ensued. The family members abroad send regular remittances and these funds were used to improve the family's homes. Makeshift houses were thus replaced with new ones, often in the same location. Some of the makeshift houses were then converted into stores and established as business ventures to support the family. In 2004 the Ministry of Finance and Economic Planning estimated that each year more than US$400 million is sent home through remittances by Ghanaians abroad, and this accounts for nearly 40 per cent of external investment. By this informal but co-operative process potential slum areas such as Nima, Sukura, Maamobi, Madina, Teshie and Chorkor have changed and improved significantly (Owusu-Achiaw, 2002).

The second factor that has accounted for the near elimination of real slum development in Accra is the World Bank Urban Renewal and Redevelopment Projects (Urban I – VI), which in the late 1980s and 1990s embarked on the development of access roads, drains, and the provision of water and sanitary services for selected slum areas in Accra including Nima, Maamobi, Sukura and Madina. As part of the Highly Indebted Poor Countries (HIPC) initiatives, substantial expenditure is going into drains and roads in a number of low-income communities in Accra and elsewhere in the country.

It must be acknowledged though, that within the Central Business District a temporary settlement of refuge seekers from an ethnic conflict in the northern part of Ghana has developed. This place is called Sodom and Gomorrah and it comes close to what could be described as a slum. The city authority has made temporary provision for social services such as water and electricity available. Plans are far advanced to remove the settlement and thus it is not worthwhile discussing it further here, although earlier attempts by city authorities to remove the illegal settlement were halted by a court injunction sponsored by a local NGO.

---

for low-income households, with 28 per cent of those surveyed citing this as a barrier to access (BiG/ASI, 2002). This finding may be corroborated with the evidence in Table 5.1 that shows that from 1999 through to 2002 it cost more than 15 per cent of average household income (41 per cent in 2002) to connect to the utility's mains.

	Table 5.1. Connection fees and GDP per capita					
Year	Average connection fee in cities (CF) - (¢)	Average connection fee in small towns (CF) - (¢)	Nominal GDP per capita - (¢)	Mean annual household income - (¢)	CF/GDP per capita (%) (small towns in brackets) 1/3(2/3)	CF/ mean annual household income (%) (small towns in brackets) 1/4(2/4)
	-1-	-2-	-3-	-4-		
1996	69,000	59,000	586,365		11.8 (10.1)	
1997	69,000	59,000	832,888		8.3 (7.1)	
1998	120,000	113,900	950,728		12.6 (12.0)	
1999	234,000	150,000	1,150,259	2,267,000	20.3 (13.0)	10.32 (6.62)
2000	245,000	230,000	1,482,172		16.5 (15.5)	
2001	300,000	250,000	2,024,436		14.8 (12.3)	
2002	1,000,000	550,000	2,421,225		41.3 (22.7)	

Source: Table reproduced from MIME Consult, 2002.

Table 5.1 demonstrates that based on the actual performance of the top 25 per cent of developing country utilities, a 'best practice' proxy for connection fees no higher than 20 per cent of annual per capita GDP may be assumed.[10] Table 5.1 indicates that before 1999 connection fees were fairly reasonable. However since 1999 the connection costs have shot up and confirm the point made by poor respondents in the BiG/ASI survey, that prohibitive connection fees are a barrier to accessibility. The fees being charged for 2002 (effective April 1, 2002) are indeed prohibitive. Note that connection fees are not regulated by the PURC.

It is also pertinent to summarize some of the findings in the study commissioned by the PURC on water accessibility (Box 5.2):

Box 5.2. Some PURC findings on water accessibility

- The majority of households in piped areas do not have primary access to piped water, despite a clear preference for and interest in accessing GWC services. Of the 60 per cent of households that do not receive piped water supply from GWC, two-thirds are classified as poor.
- The cost of connection to piped water supply is a key barrier for non-piped households; however the cost of water is less of an issue than ease of access.
- The water sources on which non-piped households (mainly the poor) rely are more expensive than piped water. The prices paid for water by source range from ¢42 per 18-litre bucket[†] (¢2330/m³) for piped water to ¢498 (¢27,667/ m³) by buckets/containers through supplies by tankers. The highest average prices paid for water from standpipes and neighbour sellers are ¢121 and ¢161 per bucket respectively. This is clear evidence that the poor are paying relatively more for water, as they are the ones who depend on neighbour sellers and tanker supplies.

[†] The standard means of dispensing water is the size 34 bucket, which contains 18 litres of water.
'Neighbour resellers' are those who are connected to the network and sell water to others who are not connected.

Source: Table reproduced from MIME Consult, 2002.

5.5 Poor people's water needs and usage

In Accra, access to water has become a key factor in choosing where to live and what rent to pay. The same property will cost less if there is no reliable water supply. It is therefore economically feasible for the poor to live in these relatively cheaper rent areas. This is at a huge cost, however, of poor access to water. This phenomenon is illustrated in Box 5.3.

The field data indicate that in poor households, the average daily requirement for water is around 180 litres (36 litres per capita). For an average household of five the water is used for cooking, washing utensils and clothes, washing, and drinking. Figure 5.1 indicates that around 30 per cent of the water used by poor households for domestic activities is for bathing for all the members of the household. On average each member of the household washes or bathes twice a day, but this is reduced to once as a coping means during the dry season, when only the children are washed twice. The next highest demand for water comes from cooking, which also uses 27 per cent in normal times. During the dry season cooking at home is reduced in favour of buying street-food, again to reduce water usage. Ironically, drinking, which is considered to be the most vital use, takes only 4 per cent of the supply of those surveyed.

Box 5.3. Interview with tenant at Lashibi

'I used to live in Ashalley Botwe, in the North-eastern part of Accra, where there is no reticulated system and residents have to depend on tankers and cart operators for their water supply. I paid ¢800,000 a month for a four-bedroom house with a garage and a boy's quarters. This was very cheap by all standards. However, I had to pay ¢500,000 to buy the equivalent of two tanker loads of water every month. If we had to buy in buckets because a tanker was not available, we paid between ¢800-1200 per bucket. Our total water consumption was 3,000 gallons (13.5 m³) for a household of five. We moved to Lashibi in the Eastern part of Accra where the water flows regularly and we are paying ¢1.2 million for a three-bedroom duplex. On balance we are better off, as we do not have to struggle to get water from tankers and our total expenditure on rent and water comes to about the same. I am currently billed an average of ¢55,000 for 15 m³ of water every month'.

This case relates to a middle-income tenant; it may not be entirely applicable to the poor as rent is likely to be the main determinant of where they choose to live.

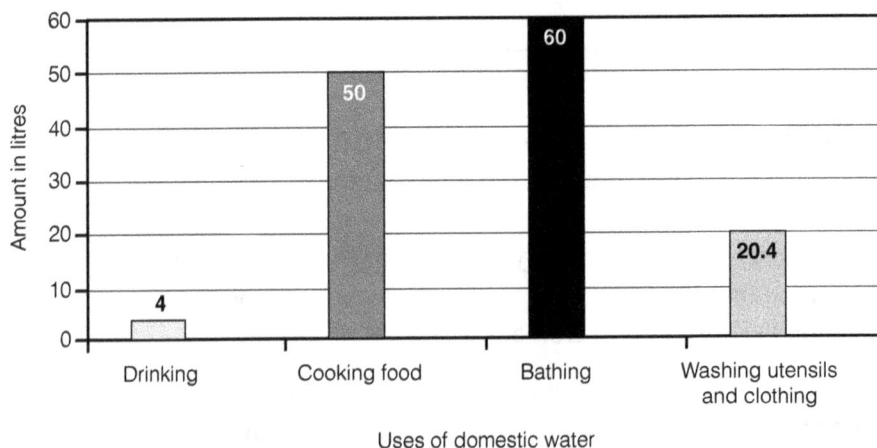

Figure 5.1. Use of water for domestic activities

5.6   Poor people's water supply systems

Poor people are likely to depend on several sources of water as a key coping process. The study revealed three major sources of water often purchased from SWEs by poor people (see Figure 5.2).

Nearly 68 per cent of respondents rely on water vendors who sell in 18-litre buckets at ¢700–¢1000. A number of them (about 20 per cent) also rely on the power tillers with tank trailers (cart operators). This is especially so in Ashalley Botwe, where some of these tillers carry 300-litre tanks and visit the neighbourhoods selling buckets directly to the households. Some of the tankers in Teshie also do the same. The information was that the tankers used to sell a little lower than the ¢700 per bucket, however due to pressure from water vendors they also had to sell at ¢700 for direct sales to consumers. It was noted that the few respondents that do not have vendors as their main source of water have them as one of their minor sources (see Figure 5.3).

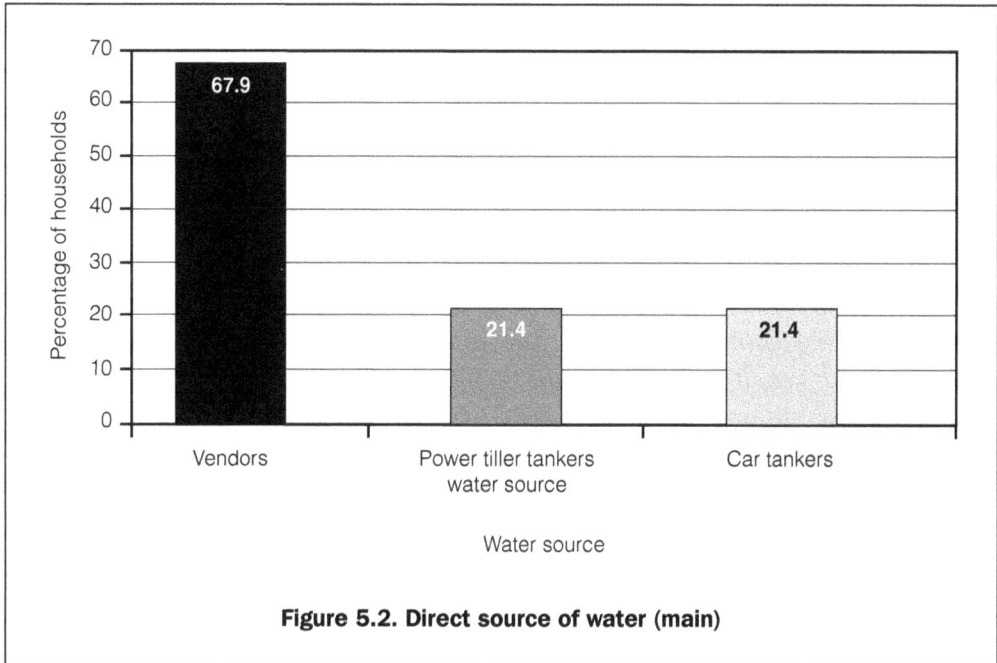

Figure 5.2. Direct source of water (main)

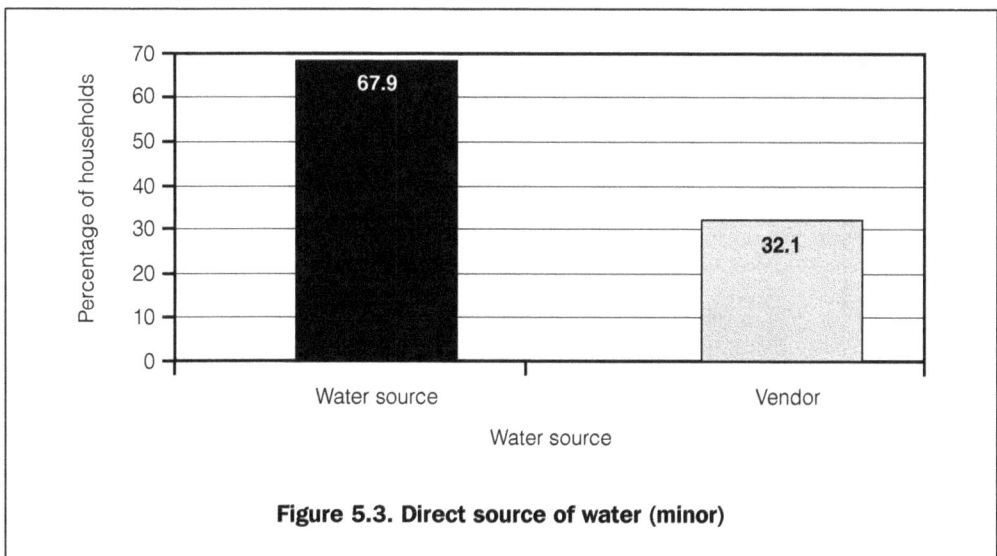

Figure 5.3. Direct source of water (minor)

5.7   Poor households' expenditure and income from water

The water element in the livelihoods of households becomes crucial if income level is assessed against expenditure. It must be noted that the poor are water sellers as well as users. The analysis of water usage indicates that at least 32 per cent of poor water-users buy water and re-bag and sell it as iced-water or iced blocks (see Figure 5.4). They are making the most of the economies of scale. As they buy large volumes of water the price is lower, and they could also be in a better situation to bargain as they control a relatively large part of their supplier's market. The survey indicates that with an average of 280 gallons used in a week and 1000 gallons purchased, the households are selling on about 720 gallons a week.

The incomes of the poor are generally low, as shown by Figure 5.5. Given the average household composition of three adults and two children, an average expenditure of ¢1,340,000 a month is moderate for a poor household.

> ".....many of us sell water to our neighbours and visitors. We often do not separate the water we buy to sell from the water we buy for domestic use, it is often difficult to define our profit but so far as we get money to replenish our stock, we deem it as profitable and more especially, it gives us a chance to negotiate with the suppliers".

> *Female household consumer.*

The typical expenditure pattern is as shown below, in Table 5.2. This shows that expenditure on water is the fourth most costly household expense and constitutes nearly 10 per cent of the monthly expenditure. This is very substantial and any change can affect the general expenditure of the poor. Table 5.3 shows the volumes of water used by different households, and the amount spent buying water.

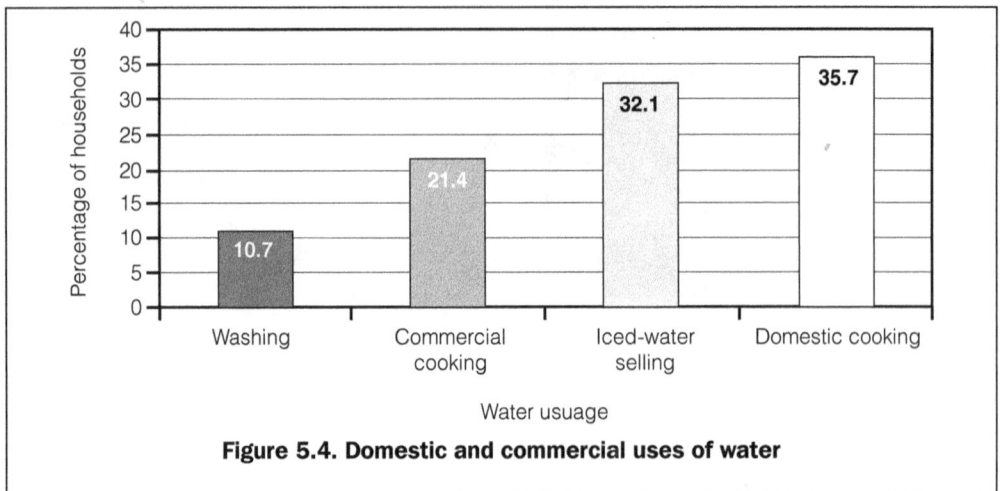

Figure 5.4. Domestic and commercial uses of water

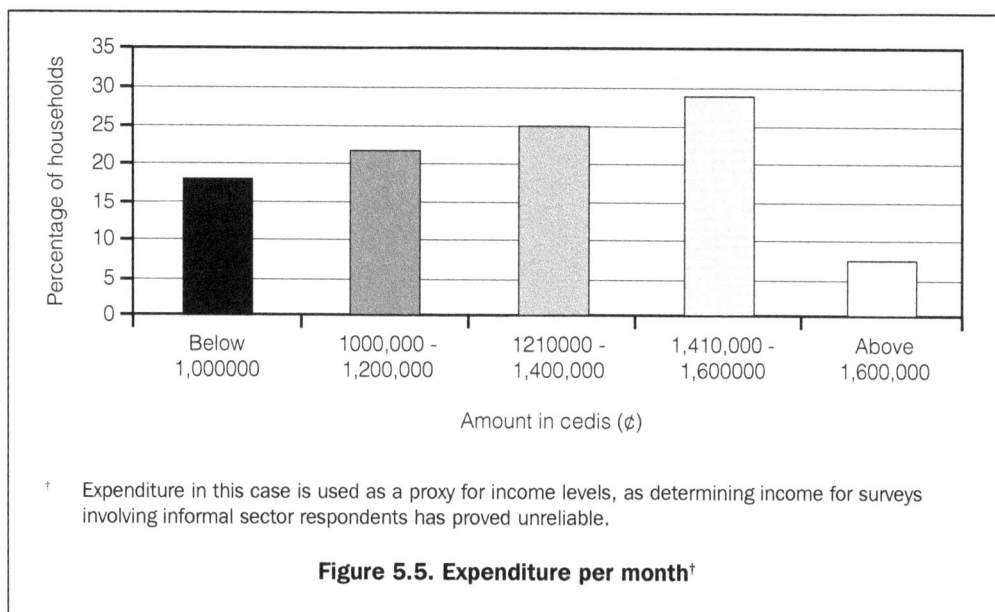

[†] Expenditure in this case is used as a proxy for income levels, as determining income for surveys involving informal sector respondents has proved unreliable.

Figure 5.5. Expenditure per month†

Table 5.2. Typical poor household expenditure pattern

Items	Amount	%	Rank
Food	600,000	42	1
Rent	350,000	25	2
Clothing	200,000	14	3
Water	100,000	9.1	4
Electricity	45,000	3.2	7
Other utilities	50,000	3.5	5
Social obligations	50,000	3.5	5
Total	**1,395,000**	**100**	

Source: Field data.

The focus group discussion revealed that despite poor people spending more than 20 per cent of their income on water, their water needs are not thoroughly met. In the dry season the situation becomes worse as the water price increases and the supplement from rainwater is also not available.

Table 5.3.	Expenditure on water per month		
Amount in litres/day	Amount spent on water	Number of households in field survey	%
120	60,000	3	10.7
160	80,000	1	3.6
180	90,000	8	28.6
200	100,000	7	25.0
240	120,000	8	28.6
260	130,000	1	3.6
Total		28	100.0

Source: Field data.

5.8 Access to water – poor people's choice

There are three major practical sources of water open to poor households in water-deprived areas of Accra. These sources are shown in Figure 5.6. Choice of source is determined by: (a) the price and payment arrangements, (b) the reliability of provision, and (c) the quality of water.

For the poor household the price and payment arrangements are the most crucial factors. This is necessary as beyond a certain price for water, it does not only take a chunk of the household's disposable income but it also becomes so lucrative that even school children and some parents sacrifice education to sell water. This is particularly the case in the sale of iced sachet water and iced blocks by young girls (along the streets) and female adults (wholesaling/retailing), which has become a common sight in Ghana's cities.[11] Any abnormal price increases in water thus have major implications for choice and livelihood patterns.

In some instances the field discussions revealed that quality is immediately sacrificed and water from nearby stagnant pools then becomes the alternative.

The means of payment is also very crucial as poor people need to buy water even when they have no money, so sources that offer credit are therefore the most attractive to the poor household.

The reliability of the supply is also crucial for the poor. In this respect vendors that are closer to households and can offer preferential treatment to neighbours in lean periods are preferred to itinerant tankers that roam neighbourhoods and sell at cheaper prices. Nevertheless price is still a key influencing factor.

The quality of the water is the last factor influencing choice of sources. The basic assumption is that the water is coming from a trusted source – GWC. The water could only be contaminated by the transporting agent. A new tanker may thus be more attractive than a rusted one, and a vendor with a new polythene storage tank may be more attractive than an underground cement tank, which is prone to seepage and contamination.

5.9 Coping strategies of poor people with respect to water

Poor people, though vulnerable in many situations, have adopted their own means of coping with situations of water deprivation. When water becomes difficult to access for poor households along the coast (including Old Teshie), the sea becomes a crucial asset. Sea-water is used for bathing thoroughly and just a few cups of fresh water are used to rinse. This applies to washing and rinsing cooking bowls as well. In another situation, water from nearby ponds is used to wash clothes and water purchased from vendors is used for rinsing.

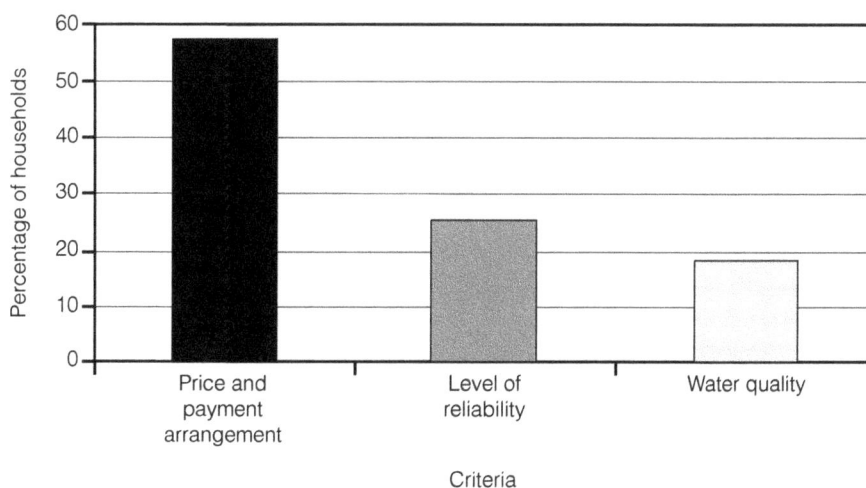

Figure 5.6. Factors influencing choice of water

One classic coping strategy observed was that in almost one out of every five houses in Teshie there is a water vendor. When there is a water shortage the vendors sell only a certain amount of their supply and keep the rest for their family and neighbours who are their close and regular customers. This ensures that even in very difficult times, people still have access to water for their domestic use.

Many of the households also conserve water by reducing the number of times they have a bath, whilst children are prioritized in the allocation of drinking water.

5.10 Water quality and health

Given the long interval between each cleaning of the tanks and vendors' reservoirs there is a high probability of contamination. This has been noted by the GWC in its investigations of causes and incidences of contamination. This was acknowledged by all tanker operators and domestic vendors as well, and they conceded that there is no established means of assessing water quality.[12] The PURC and GWC are currently in discussions with the tanker associations on the establishment of guidelines to ensure the quality of water delivered to consumers.

Most operators assess water quality by observing its colour, usually while it is being dispensed to the vendor or consumer. Around 80 per cent of consumers also judge their water quality by its colour. Some also smell or drink the water to check for chlorine, to prove that it is from a GWC source. This is woefully inadequate.

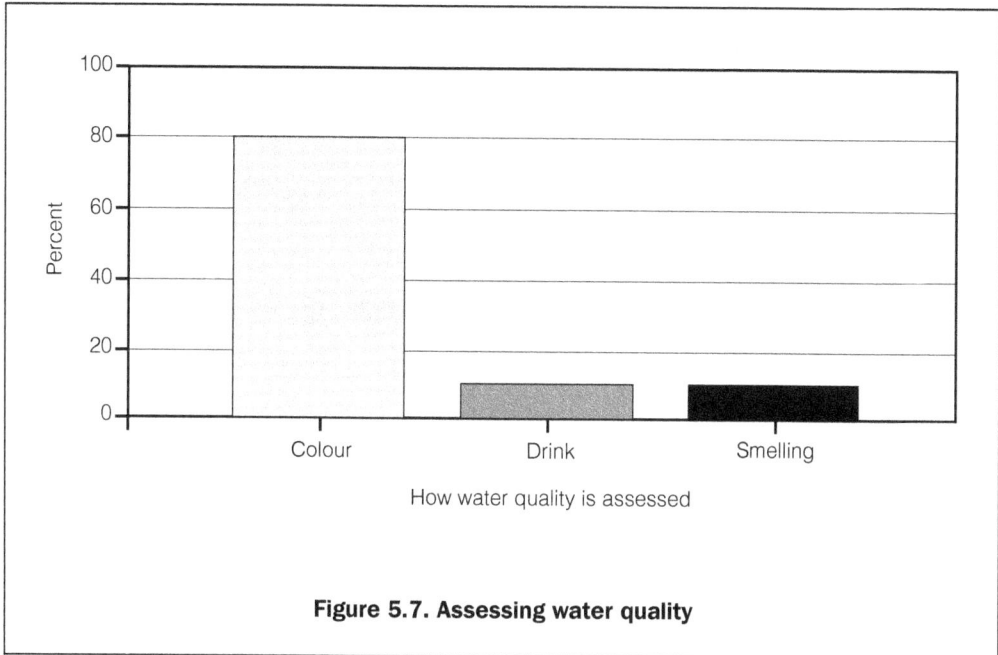

Figure 5.7. Assessing water quality

9. It should be mentioned here that the World Bank now uses the Gross National Income (GNI) and quotes $270 for Ghana in most of its documents (see Project Appraisal Document for Urban Water Supply Credit for Ghana, 2004).

10. Online discussion hosted by Nicola Tynan and Bill Kingdom on 'A Scorecard for Water Utilities in Developing Countries', Jan-Feb 2002. One could argue that the use of household income, rather than GDP per capita, is more appropriate, as there is only one water supply connection for the whole household. Note that the mean household income would be roughly twice as much as GDP per capita in the unlikely event that both spouses in a household may actually be earning income.

11. The sale of iced water in plastic sachets has come under tremendous attack in recent years because of its environmental impact. Accra city authorities have sought to impose a heavy levy on sachet water producers to enable them to clear the city of the plastic menace. This has met with considerable resistance and the city authorities have threatened to ban the sale of water in sachets. This would have tremendous impact on the livelihoods of a number of poor people, particularly women and children.

12. This came out in the focus group discussions and in the stakeholders' workshop as well.

Chapter 6

Small Water Enterprises (general)

6.1 Introduction

This chapter introduces small water enterprises (SWE) and describes their characteristics, operations, and finally their constraints and the potential they have to provide water for poor households in informal communities.

6.2 Role and functions of SWEs

GWC records indicate that nearly 43 per cent of households in Accra are not served directly, or are underserved (GWC). The unserved/underserved consumers have to rely on other providers for water, and SWEs have become the default suppliers. As the chairman of one tanker association puts it:

"We are not mere charlatans selling water to unfortunate needy households for money, far from that; we are performing a critical social role of giving access to water to needy communities and helping the government to met a critical social responsibility."

Tanker operator.

This statement shows how operators perceive their role in the water sector.

6.3 Types and characteristics of SWEs

SWEs in Accra are always innovating so fixed definitions do not apply for long, however six major categories of SWEs have been identified during the study. These are:

- water tanker operators (who transport water in bulk)
- motorized cart operators (power tiller tankers)
- domestic vendors who obtain their water from tankers, and sell water to neighbours
- GWC direct-supplied vendors (neighbour sellers and kiosks)

- sachet-water sellers and producers
- street water sellers

In addition there is an emerging group of providers who provide water from their own source to the end-user and who may be described as 'mini utilities' (MIME, 2002). They do not have reticulated systems but sell directly from the source to customers or to tankers. In the north of the city of Accra – where groundwater is less saline – a number of individuals have sunk boreholes to abstract water both for their own use and to sell on.

Below we discuss the different types of SWEs.

Water tanker operators

This describes an ordinary vehicle with a tank fixed to it. The size of the tank ranges from 1200 to 3500 gallons. In exceptional cases 4000 to 4500-gallon tanks are used. The tankers are owned by individuals, but for operational purposes they have formed associations. In Accra there are currently five major associations operating, and all these have a formal relationship with the GWC. There are other operators as well (see Table 6.1).

Table 6.1. Water tanker services in Accra

Tanker association	No. of tankers	Areas served
Private Water Tanker Owners' Association (PWTOA) – Accra	300	Kasoa and Bortianor area (Accra West)
Odorkor Tanker Owners' Association	10	Odorkor (Accra West)
Madina Water Tanker Owners'/Drivers' Association	50	Madina, Ashongman, Ashalley Botwe, Adenta, Frafraha
Lashibi Tanker Association	150	Labadi, Teshie & Nungua, Batsoona, Sakumono, Ashiaman, Tema
Sakaman	10	Bortianor, Odorkor (western part of Accra)
Labour Enterprise Trust (LET)	4	Eastern Accra
Ghana Water Company	4	Not specified (however mostly eastern Accra)

The associations have become the organizing points for the tankers and they negotiate on behalf of their members. They also negotiate for the hydrant filling point from the utility and it is available only to their members, who also pay the meter-recorded tariff every fortnight. The tankers do not discriminate among customers. Limitations to serving particular communities may be a result of distance and other economic considerations rather than an imposition.

Motorized cart operators (power-tiller tankers)

These carts are made from motorized power tillers that were actually imported into the country for agricultural purposes. Normally one would fix a plough to the rear of these tillers for farming purposes, but innovative entrepreneurs have instead fixed carts mounted with 300-gallon tanks. Pumps have been attached to facilitate the drawing of water from domestic vendors (the most common situation) and from the utility's mains. Some of these powered carts belong to the tanker associations but, as the survey showed, many of them are itinerant and do not even have fixed customers.

This category of SWEs has no formal relationship with GWC, but where they belong to a tanker association they are able to source water directly from the utility's filling points.

Photograph 6.1. Cart operator in Ashalley Botwe

Photograph © K.S.Mann (MIME Consult)

Tanker-supplied domestic vendors

Domestic vendors are located within the communities and have underground storage tanks or polythene tanks. Their storage volume ranges from 1000 to 5000 gallons. Water is bought from tankers and sold in 18-litre buckets or 20-litre containers directly to households. In some cases vendors originally built the tanks for their own home storage and then, due to pressure from neighbours, these were turned into commercial operations. The operators are mostly women who are often on low incomes and rely on this as a main livelihood source.

GWC direct-supplied vendors (neighbour sellers and kiosks)

This category of vendor is different from the former mainly due to the source of water. They depend on water from the GWC mains. These vendors operate in areas that are usually served, although they sometimes supplement their supplies with tankered water when the GWC supply is unavailable. This type of vendor has proliferated in low-income communities because:

- some households are unable to pay the connection fee to hook up to the utility's grid, so they depend on neighbour sellers;
- water vending, with its associated payment arrangements, favours the poor; and

Photograph © K.S.Mann (MIME Consult)

Photograph 6.2. Tanker serving a vendor

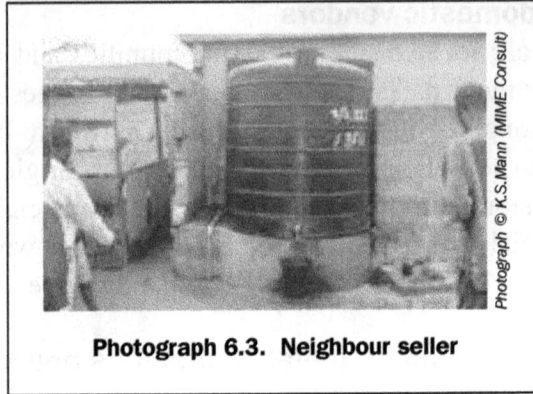

Photograph 6.3. Neighbour seller

- due to pressure differences, some more affluent members of the community in low-pressure areas 'trap' the water in huge reservoirs before it can flow to those higher up, and then re-sell to those living on higher ground[13] (some landlords also deliberately set these up due to frequent problems associated with bill payments where one bill has to be shared among several tenants in a dwelling).

The GWC says that they do not recognize domestic vendors as these vendors are partly to blame for the inability of some residents to get their supply. It is ironic however, that in most cases these vendors are charged commercial rates (instead of domestic), signifying a contractual relationship.

Water-sachet producers

Water-sachet producers are the latest form of SWEs. Street water sellers in Ghana used to sell water in cups but the Municipal Authorities banned this to safeguard people's health. The sellers then shifted to putting the water in transparent plastic bags, tying them up and selling. This was also considered unhygienic (studies by the Ghana Standards Board actually confirmed this) and as suspicion about the water quality grew, many consumers stopped buying. Then some entrepreneurs imported machines to filter the water and put it in sealed sachets. This immediately caught on with the consuming public, as it was deemed much more acceptable. In a way, the proliferation of water-sachet sellers is an indication of the lack of public confidence in the water supplied by GWC, even though there is evidence that most of the water-sachets contain water of lower quality than that of the utility.[14] The water for the sachets is either from a tanker or directly from the utility's mains, and is then filtered and sealed in the polythene plastic.

The producers have formed an Association of Sachet Water Producers to fight for the rights of their members.

Street water sellers

This is the lowest level of selling water-sachets. Many of the sellers are women, young girls and children from poor households, or home-helps from high-income homes. Selling water in the street has become a real business for many poor homes and the best means of getting potable water for the households and individuals. A casual observation of street sellers at traffic intersections indicates that young men are more interested in selling other wares, whilst the girls sell water.

6.4   Water supply chain

The general water supply chain in Accra (and many of the urban areas in Ghana) is shown in Figure 6.1. The figure shows that in Accra all potable water sources emanate from the utility. It is only in the next stage of the chain that the SWEs participate by distributing to consumer. The utility is SWEs' main source, and after that come tankers and domestic vendors or neighbour sellers. In unserved communities tankers often supply water directly to domestic vendors. Commercial users (including water-sachet producers and the bulk iced-water sellers) also buy directly from the tanker operators, although in most cases they also depend on GWC sources. The tanker operators also supply cart operators, who buy in quantities of about 300 gallons. Those who need water for construction purposes also buy from the tanker operators. In the high-income areas, households buy directly from tanker operators.

Domestic vendors who depend on the tankers mainly supply households for domestic use. There are, however, a few customers who buy for commercial purposes such as for food processing, bulk iced-water production, iced-water retailing, and small construction activities. The motorized cart operators very often supply middle to low-income homes that have storage. At the end of the provider's chain are street and kiosk iced-water sellers, and the consumers are pedestrians and households.

It is significant to note that storage capacity determines the buyer and the seller's discharge quantity. Different customers will have different storage volumes, and this will influence their choice of water supplier. For a poor household the maximum purchase is in buckets, thus they can only afford to buy small volumes of water from a domestic vendor, while a high-income household could purchase from a tanker or a cart, whose unit price (price per gallon) is much cheaper. The economies of scale thus simply work their way down the chain.

Poor households depend on four main chains for their water supply. These are presented in Table 6.2 and include observations as well as findings from the survey. Note that in Table 6.2 the term 'kiosks' applies to various categories of people

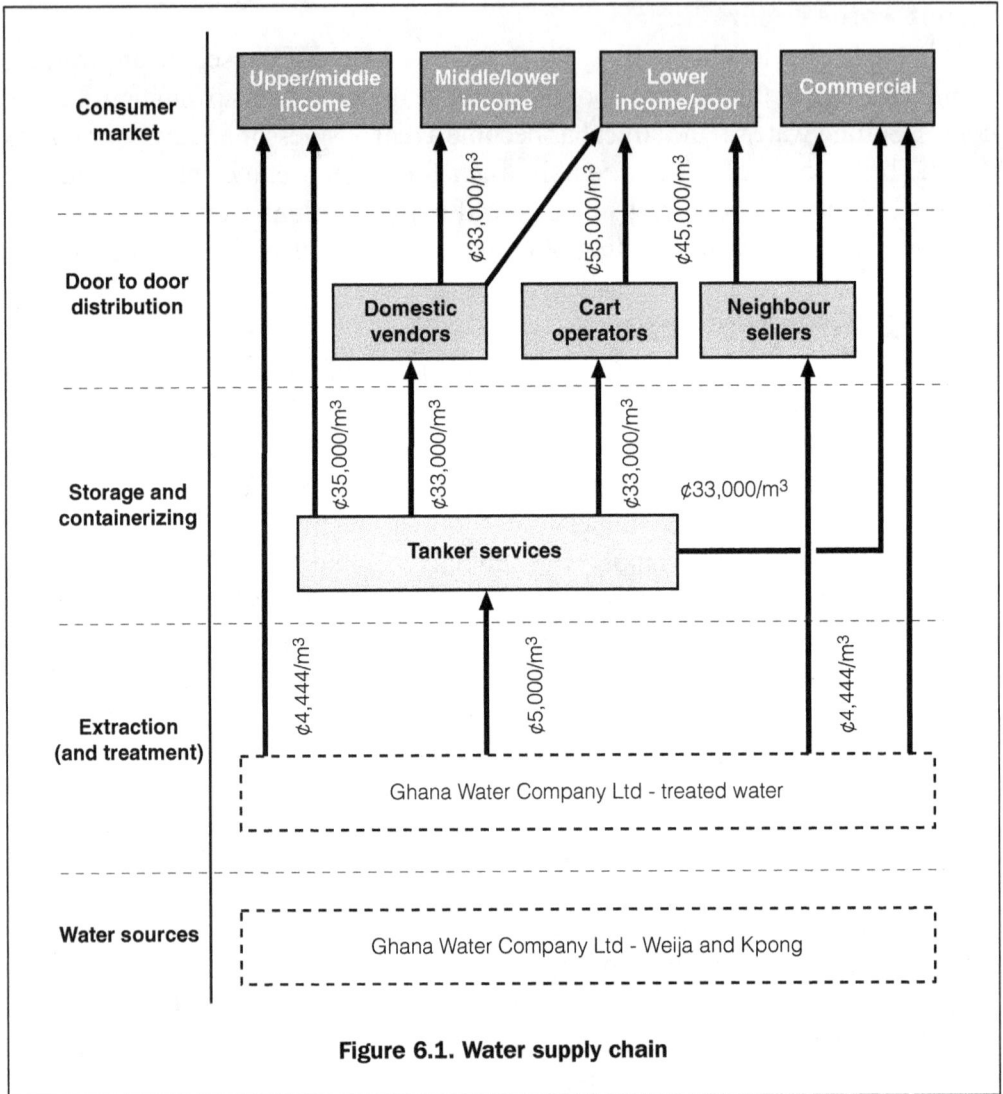

Figure 6.1. Water supply chain

Consumer market

Upper/middle income | Middle/lower income | Lower income/poor | Commercial

¢33,000/m³ ¢55,000/m³ ¢45,000/m³

Door to door distribution

Domestic vendors | Cart operators | Neighbour sellers

Storage and containerizing

¢35,000/m³ ¢33,000/m³ ¢33,000/m³ ¢33,000/m³

Tanker services

Extraction (and treatment)

¢4,444/m³ ¢5,000/m³ ¢4,444/m³

Ghana Water Company Ltd - treated water

Water sources

Ghana Water Company Ltd - Weija and Kpong

Figure 6.1. Water supply chain

who sell water to neighbours, whether they are supplied with water from tankers and store water in tanks, or get their water directly from the water distribution network.

The table indicates that the most dependable channel for poor households in normal and shortage periods is the service from the network through the tankers and a kiosk and to households. The second most dependable channel in periods of shortage is the network through a kiosk (vendor), through cart operators, then to households. During the dry season and water shortage periods the two channels that are most dependable are from the network through the tankers and a kiosk and to households, and from the network to kiosks and cart operators to households.

Table 6.2. Dependence on SWEs (by type)

Description	Source by % during normal times	Source by % during shortage periods	Rank by importance during normal times	Rank by importance during shortage periods	Bottlenecks and inefficiencies
Network → tanker → kiosk → household	70	95	1st	1st	Quality concerns raised due to multi-level handling Longer chain implies high prices
Network → cart operator → household	8	0	3rd	-	Limited in scope as there are no indicated filling points Quality concerns
Network → kiosk → cart operator → household	20	5	2nd	2nd	Limited by water rationing in areas where chain operates Multi-level handling raises price and quality concerns
Network → kiosk → household	2	0	4th	-	Limited by water rationing in areas where chain operates

The presentation and the analysis indicates that any attempt to respond to the water needs of the poor must consider the key partners in the chain – the tankers, vendors, and the cart operators.

6.5 Price share in the water supply chain

The following relative prices as at April 2004 were observed (see Table 6.3).

Table 6.3 indicates that neighbour sellers (who take water from the utility and resell it to others) may make the greatest profit (68 per cent), compared to the others in the supply chain, because they do not have the costs associated with running and maintaining a tanker. Tanker and cart deliveries similarly keep a large percentage of the cost of delivered water, but this is not surprising given the transport element in their operations. By far the worst affected in the supply chain, in terms of price, are the customers who are not connected to the network and who depend on water

Table 6.3. Price share in the cost of water to consumer

	Final price to consumer	% to cart operator	% to domestic vendor (kiosk)	% to neighbour-seller (kiosk)	% to tanker	% to utility
Network → household (poor)	¢4,444/m³					100
Network → kiosk → household	¢13,900/m³			68		32
Network → tanker → household	¢35,000/m³				86	14
Network → tanker → kiosk → household	¢55,000/m³		40		51	9
Network → kiosk → cart operator → household	¢45,000/m³	69	21			10

Note
Prices at each point in the chain are based on survey findings, rates supplied by GWCL, and PURC approved tariffs.

purchased from domestic vendors who are supplied by tankers. These mainly poor people pay as much as ¢55,000/m³ or – more appropriately – ¢1,000/bucket for their water. In terms of quality, they are also likely to be the worst affected, given that their water is being handled at three different levels before it reaches their household: the utility, the tanker, and the vendor.

In the next chapter we discuss the operations of the various SWEs.

---

13. Based on discussions with ATMA Regional Manager, Accra East.

14. This is based on water quality analysis carried out by Esi Awua, a Senior Lecturer at the Kwame Nkrumah University of Science and Technology. The report is yet to be published.

Chapter 7

Small Water Enterprises (tankers)

7.1 Introduction

It is important, in the Ghanaian situation, to have a good understanding of the evolution and general operating environment of tankers. This is so because, as was shown in Chapter 6, other key SWEs like vendors and neighbour sellers depend heavily on selling on bulk supplies from tankers. The slightest change in tanker operations therefore affects the operations of other SWEs down the chain, with consequent impacts on poor consumers. Therefore a substantial part of these discussions is based on tanker operations, because of the key role played by tankers. In addition tankers are the SWEs that have an officially recognized relationship with the utility, even though other SWEs play significant roles in the distribution chain.

7.2 Tankers – historical perspective

Tanker operations first emerged as a means to provide water for construction activities. The need for potable water in unserved areas became so alarming in the late 1980s, however, that tankers began to distribute potable water. The tankers were at first 'stealing' water from Fire Service hydrant points and selling it. To resolve this problem the utility established filling points in selected locations in Accra. Water tanker associations were formed to bring some order to the filling operations. At the time, the GWC also operated its own tankers to both supply areas without water and deal with emergency situations.

7.3 Organization of tanker associations

Tanker operators are organized into various associations. Membership of the individual associations is open to all owners of water tankers and water tanker drivers. The registration process begins with a registration form listing simple personal and professional records. Tanker owners pay a registration fee of ¢300,000 and drivers only ¢10,000. The Lashibi Association is made up of about 300 members with 150 tankers. The Madina Association has about 100 members with 50 tankers.

There are three kinds of operators in the tanker associations: (a) tanker owners, (b) drivers, and (c) owner-drivers. Membership is skewed towards owners, as shown in Figure 7.1.

There are five active tanker associations in Accra. They are all young – formed less than 10 years ago – with an average length of membership of 4.5 years. Membership is obligatory for those working in the business, as it is the only means of controlling and ensuring discipline. The association leaders are elected for three years and the associations are registered as affiliate members of the Trades Union Congress through the Ghana Private Road Transport Union.

7.4   Fleet and resources

One striking thing about the tanker operations is that their major resource is the vehicles. Unfortunately the vehicles are very old (from a sample of 20 vehicles many were more than 20 years old – see Table 7.1). Consequently they break down frequently. Running costs are also high, thus affecting reliability and operating costs.

The analysis revealed a very strong correlation between the cost of operation and age of vehicle. The vehicles are ordinarily very good makes, including well-known names such as Benz, DAF and Leyland. Some of the vehicles are built by cannibalizing old trucks.

Table 7.1. Average age of tankers			
Vehicle type	**Age (years)**	**Number of carts or tankers**	**%**
Motorized carts	Less than 10	3	15.0
Tankers	10 – 20	6	30.0
Tankers	21 – 30	8	40.0
Tankers	More than 30	3	15.0
		20	100.0

Field survey sample size: 20.

7.5 Supply of water to tankers

The filling of tankers is well regulated by the full-time staff employed by the associations. Each vehicle registers, joins a queue and waits its turn to be filled. A down payment is required before water is supplied, even though the associations themselves are billed fortnightly by the utility. The rates charged at the filling points for different sizes of tankers are shown in Figure 7.2. There is an additional fee of ¢5,000 per fill-up to meet the administrative costs of the filling point.

Under the arrangements between the Lashibi Tankers Association and the GWC, members fill up four days in the week and only between 6.00am to 6.00pm. When

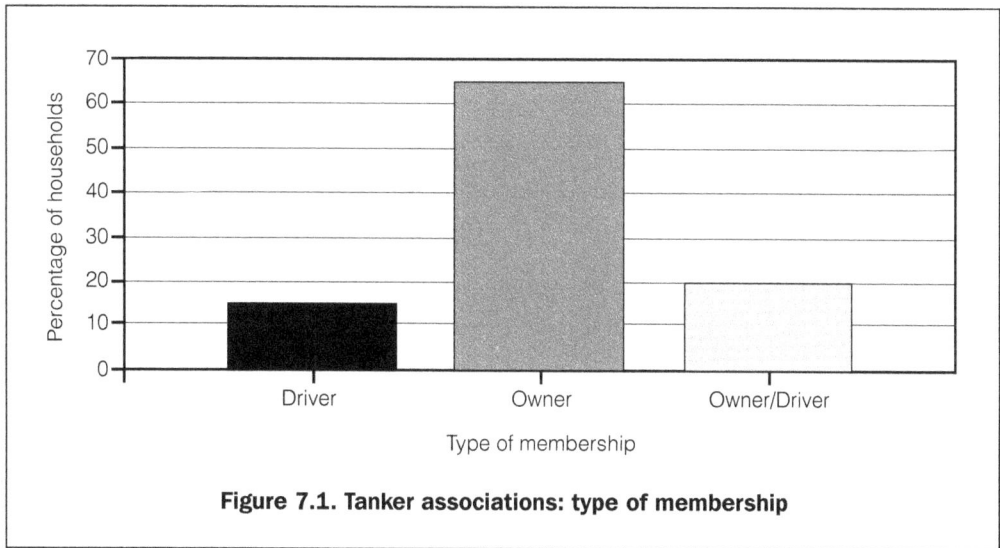

Figure 7.1. Tanker associations: type of membership

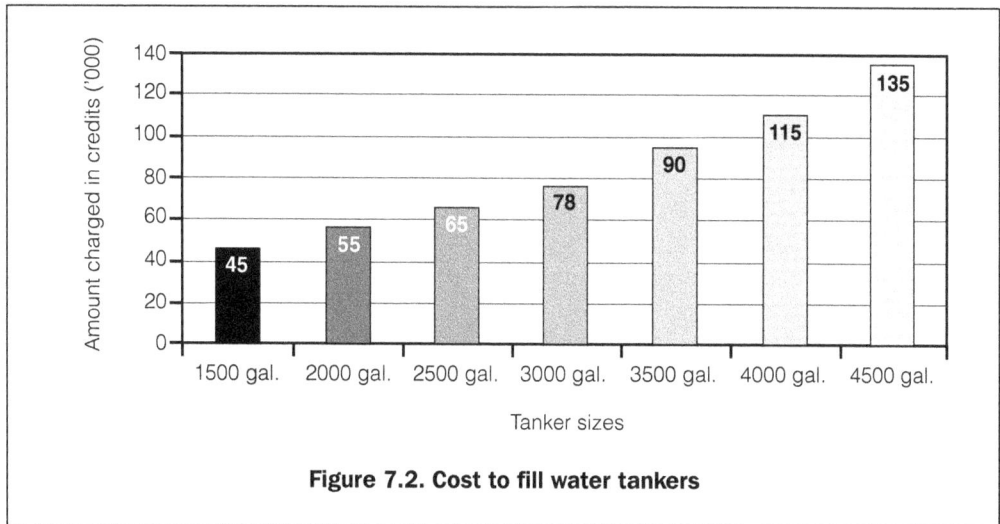

Figure 7.2. Cost to fill water tankers

the pressure is good it takes about 10 minutes to fill a 2,500-gallon tanker. When the pressure is low pressure it can take more than 30 minutes to fill the same tank. On average, tankers fill up twice a day, or eight times a week.

The members consider 'access to water' to be the most crucial element in their operation. Ironically this is also the most disappointing element, as members can spend up to six hours waiting for their turn at the filling points.

7.6   Reaching the customer

The tanker associations consider the customer to be the most important element in the whole process. The tankers have just a few direct customers, even though there are a lot more customers along the supply chain who (indirectly) depend on them. The assessment by 20 tanker operators of the customer ranking in their business is presented in Tables 7.2 to 7.4.

The tables indicate that the tankers' key customers are vendors, who account for 85 per cent of their first-ranked customers. This is followed by services to individual households, often in the high-income areas. There are also significant

Table 7.2.   Customer type ranked 1st by tankers

Rank	Customer type	Frequency	%
1	Vendors	17	85
2	Individual households	3	15
	Total	**20**	**100**

Table 7.3.   Customer type ranked 2nd by tankers

Rank	Customer type	Frequency	%
1	Vendors	7	35
2	Water-sachet producers	6	30
3	Construction services	5	25
4	Individual households	2	10
	Total	**20**	**100**

Table 7.4.	Customer type ranked 3rd by tankers		
Rank	**Customer type**	**Frequency**	**%**
	Not applicable	6	30
1	Construction services	9	45
2	Water-sachet producers	3	15
3	Vendors	2	10
	Total	**20**	**100**

services to construction activities as well as water-sachet producers.[15] The finding that vendors are the predominant customers of tankers is important, as it runs counter to the popular perception that tankers only serve the rich.

There were three main ways for the customer to reach the tanker operator for services. These are: (a) direct contact and arrangement at the filling point; (b) calls to the drivers on cell phones; and (c) regular arrangements to which the tanker operator responds.

Many vendors follow the tankers to the filling point and then guide them to their location. This happens because if demand is high and a vendor/customer is prepared to pay a little higher than the recommended price, the operator will probably divert the product. High-income customers will often pay enough that a telephone call is sufficient to secure service.

The operators also establish customer bonds with some of their clients. This, according to the operators, happens because some customers offer them credit to help maintain their vehicles and meet other business expenses. These customers receive priority services and are supplied at regular intervals. The tankers always try to keep a variety of customers from different income groups and locations to keep a broad customer base for their business.

7.7   Pricing and competition

Recommended tanker rates

The setting of water prices is crucial and the key decision-making factor in this demand-based business. The tanker associations are given recommended prices, which are established in agreement with the utility. Recommended prices as at March 2003 are presented in Table 7.5.

| Tanker capacity (gallons) | Miles radius | | | | | |
| | 10 miles | | | 11-15 miles | | |
	Freight (Transport costs)	Water	Total	Freight (Transport costs)	Water	Total
1500	122,500	33,750	156,250	142,100	33,750	175,850
2000	154,000	45,000	199,000	177,800	45,000	222,800
2500	171,500	56,250	227,750	199,500	56,250	255,750
3000	217,000	67,500	284,500	261,800	67,500	329,300
3500	248,500	78,750	327,250	300,300	78,750	379,050
4000	308,000	90,000	398,000	336,000	90,000	426,000
4500	343,700	101,250	444,950	403,900	101,250	505,150
5000	380,800	112,500	493,300	473,200	112,500	585,700

Table 7.5. Recommended tanker rates (March 2003) in cedis

Source: Ghana Water Company.

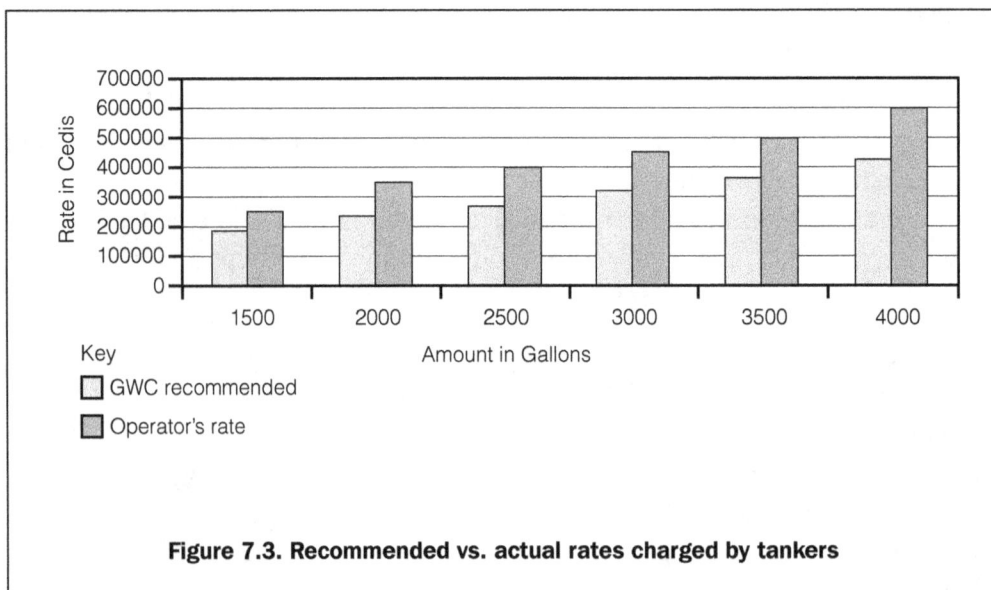

Figure 7.3. Recommended vs. actual rates charged by tankers

Table 7.5 reveals that the actual cost of water is between 19-25% of the total cost of delivered water.[16]

Figure 7.3 compares the utility's recommended prices and those charged by the operators. It is clear that in most cases the Association's members charge more than 10 per cent above what is recommended.

The GWC also has a few tankers (only four in service at the time of the report) for delivering water to unserved areas. Because there are so few tankers, the service is mostly restricted to emergency cases and to a privileged few customers. Through its business the Labour Enterprise Trust (LET), the Trades Union Congress also runs some tankers with a mission to help 'working people who face water supply problems to get water at the most viable cost'.[17] Their rates are slightly below those charged by the associations even though they are in the business to make a profit.

Figure 7.4 provides an illustration of the rates charged by GWC tankers and private tankers for tanker sizes of 1,500 and 2000 gallons, within a 10 km radius of the source.

The difference between the GWC recommended prices and those of the private associations ranges from 10 to 25 per cent. The private operators' rates are actually determined through bargaining with the customer, so the actual price paid will depend on the customer's bargaining strength. At the moment there is no established mechanism for enforcing the recommended price of the GWC. The price list is displayed at the filling point, but it at best serves as a guide.

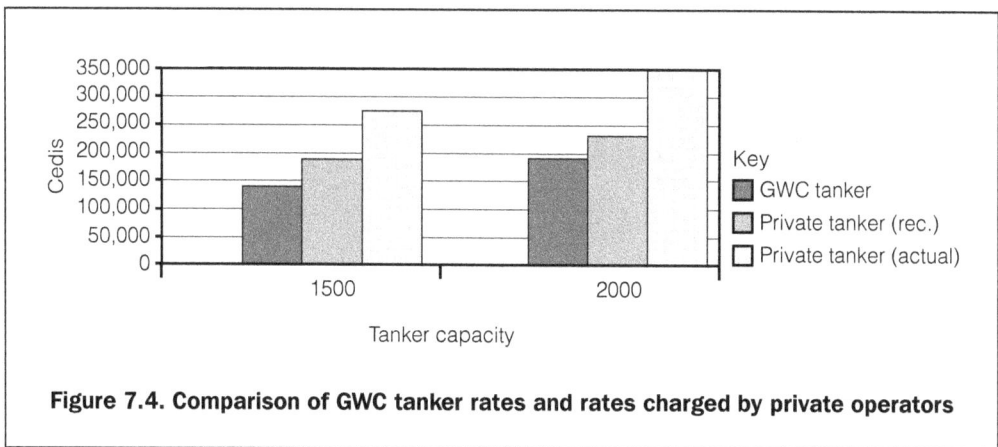

Figure 7.4. Comparison of GWC tanker rates and rates charged by private operators

Box 7.1. Operations of Labour Enterprise Trust

The Labour Enterprise Trust (LET) is a business venture established by the Trades Union Congress of Ghana. Water tankering is one of the ventures that they have moved into. The aim is to deliver water to low-income working class people at the most viable cost.

The Trust purchased new trucks for the tanker service and has been operating them for four years. The following observations were made during discussions with the General Manager, who has a grim picture of the trade. The discussion revealed that:

- The GWC tariff to the tanker operators is considered to be too high and he suggested that it should be at most equal to the domestic rate for water consumption.
- The service was described as not being a viable investment due to the high cost of repairs and maintenance of the vehicles. Tyres are changed every 10 months and cost ¢18 million for six tyres.
- The devaluation of the cedi has resulted in high interest on the initial capital investment, which is in dollars.
- The LET's rates are above those recommended by the GWC but below those charged by the private tanker associations.

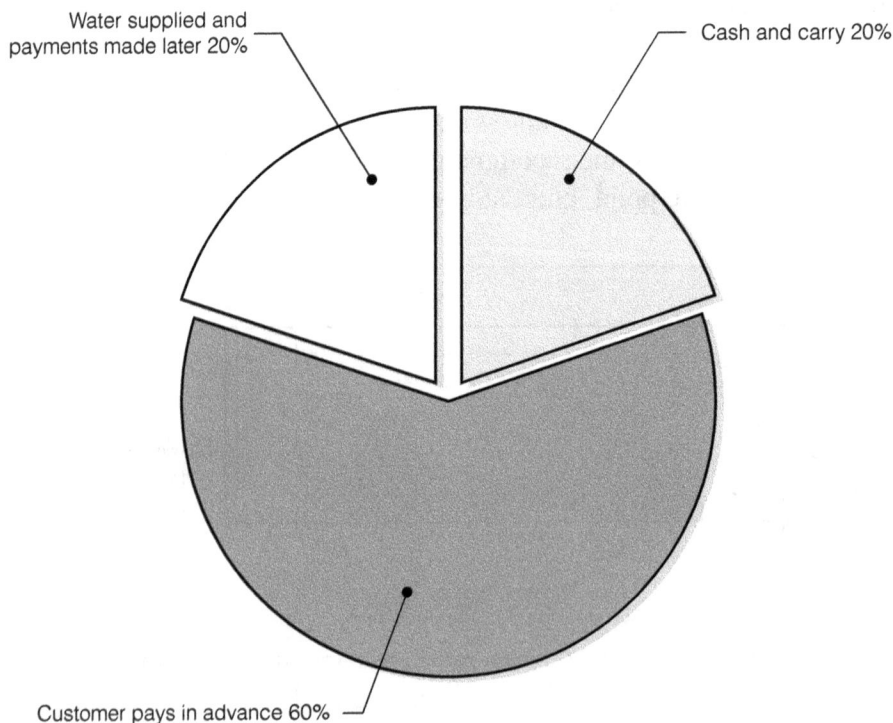

Water supplied and payments made later 20%

Cash and carry 20%

Customer pays in advance 60%

Figure 7.5. Payment arrangements for tankers

Payment arrangements

The tanker operators have adopted all sorts of means to help their various customers make their payments. Figure 7.5 depicts the payment options adopted by tanker operators. Payment in advance of delivery is most common, with similar numbers of customers paying when water is delivered and paying at a later date after delivery.

Competition

While the customers compete amongst themselves to offer the best price to attract the tanker operators, the operators have created a cartel that controls prices and supply. The tankers indicated that tanker operators compete with each other for business, and profits depend on the overhead costs for individual tankers. The motorized cart operators also sell a little more cheaply than the tanker operators, but according to the tanker operators this does not in anyway affect their operations because there is still excess demand.

7.8   Viability of tanker operations

As stated earlier, there is no doubt that there is a good market for water tanker services in the selected study communities. The viability of tanker operations is very dependent on the number of trips that can be made in a day, however, and the number of days during which water can be collected. The current critical limiting factor is access to water for selling on. Recent management actions taken by the utility have created difficulties in access, and consequently for the profitability of tanker operations. Until recently, for example, the Lashibi Tanker Association was operating six days a week. The utility has now cut this to four. Given the large number of members, tankers have to queue for several hours before they are filled. At the moment tankers are averaging only two trips a day. Although tankers have adopted some coping strategies to deal with this state of affairs,[18] the viability of the business has been greatly hampered by this decision.

Presented below is an attempt to develop the cost/revenue profile and profitability ratios for the different operating regimes.

Rate of return analyses (see scenarios 1 – 4 in Tables 7.6 to 7.9 inclusive) suggest that the profitability of the business is very sensitive to both the:

- number of operating days; and
- level of debt servicing.

Most operators do not keep records, so it is very difficult for them to assess their business performance. Analysis of the business indicates that operation in the present circumstances of curtailed filling arrangements is hardly viable. The tanker operators said that the viability of their operations is affected by the long waiting period at the filling point (which in itself could be attributed to an oversupply of vehicles, given the supply situation), the high operating costs due to the age of the trucks, and the restricted number of working days and hours.

Discussions with the chairman of the Private Water Tanker Association point to the fact that a number of tanker operators are unable to expand their operations, barely make a profit, and cannot afford to replace their vehicles when they totally break down.[19] This picture is not very different from other transport operators in Ghana. One of the principal reasons given by business analysts is the fact that in most cases entrepreneurs do not separate their private expenditures from the business, and monies accruing to the operations are often appropriated to other uses. Therefore working capital is often eroded.

7.9   Opportunities for tanker operations

Further understanding and appreciation could be had by analysing the opportunities and potential of the tanker operations.

Capacity and capabilities

Existence of formidable associations

Almost all the tanker owners and even drivers belong to an association. The association has become a focal point for negotiating on behalf of its members. The association negotiates with the utility and municipal authorities to develop hydrant supply points; it also negotiates for proposed water prices. It regulates and controls the supply of water to its members and ensures the quality of the water, although there are no arrangements for monitoring water quality, whether independently or by tanker operators. It also serves as a potential pressure group for influencing policies and regulations.

Average experience of eight years in operation

Tanker operators have been in the business for on average eight and up to sixteen years. This indicates that many of the operators have accumulated experience that could be galvanized for running the business. The long years of experience indicate that many of the operators have settled in the business and are stable enough to anticipate risks and manage them.

Recognized leadership selected by general election

The tanker associations' leaders are recognized by their membership and their decisions are accepted and acknowledged. This huge potential underlines the confidence one can have in dealing with both the leadership and the association.

Table 7.6. Scenario 1. Return on capital employed – ROCE (without financial charges)

Assumptions
a) Cost of tanker: ¢150 million for a 3,000-gallon tanker
b) Six working days per week

A. Operating Costs

Item	Cost/month	Annual
Water @¢80,000 per trip for two trips/day	3,840,000	46,080,000
Fuel @¢80,000/trip	3,840,000	46,080,000
Driver's salary @¢700,000/month	700,000	8,400,000
Allowance @¢20,000/day	480,000	5,760,000
Tax	83,333	1,000,000

A1. Repairs, maintenance and replacement

Item	Cost/month	Annual
Repairs and maintenance	2,250,000	27,000,000
Tyres replaced every year		21,000,000
A2. Total operating cost		**155,320,000**

A3. Depreciation

Annual depreciation (over five years)	2,500,000	30,000,000
B. Total Cost		**185,320,000**
C. Revenue		
Water sales – two trips/day @¢450,000	21,600,000	259,200,000
D. Total Profit/(Loss)		**73,880,000**

Return On Capital Employed (ROCE)   = $\dfrac{\text{Net Profit} \times 100}{\text{Opening Capital}}$

ROCE   = $\dfrac{73,880,000 \times 100}{150,000,000}$

     = **49.2 %**

The analysis assumes that Opening Capital came from the investor's own savings or earnings from other businesses therefore no direct financial charges are paid out of the operation. (This indeed is the case for most investors in the business.) An ROCE ratio of 49.2% as shown above, is indicative of a fairly profitable business.

Table 7.7. Scenario 2. Return on capital employed (with financial charges)

Assumptions
a) Cost of tanker – ¢150 million for a 3,000-gallon tank
b) Six working days per week

We here assume that the investor's opening capital was solely sourced from the banks and therefore debt-servicing is done out of tanker operations at a current interest rate of 30% (fixed quantum)

A. Operating Costs		
Item	**Cost/month**	**Annual**
Water @¢80,000 per trip for two trips/day	3,840,000	46,080,000
Fuel @¢80,000/trip	3,840,000	46,080,000
Driver's salary @¢700,000/month	700,000	8,400,000
Allowance @¢20,000/day	480,000	5,760,000
Tax	83,333	1,000,000
Bank Interest @ 30%	3,750,000	45,000,000
A1. Repairs, maintenance and replacement		
Item	**Cost/month**	**Annual**
Repairs and maintenance	2,250,000	27,000,000
Tyres replaced every year		21,000,000
A2. Total operating cost		**200,320,000**
A3. Depreciation		
Annual depreciation (over five years)	2,500,000	30,000,000
B. Total Cost		**230,320,000**
C. Revenue		
Water sales – two trips/day @¢450,000	21,600,000	259,200,000
D. Total Profit/(Loss)		**28,880,000**

ROCE $= \dfrac{\text{Net Profit x 100}}{\text{Opening Capital}}$

$= \dfrac{28,880,000 \times 100}{150,000,000}$

$= $ **19.2 %**

As shown above this scenario gives ROCE ratio of 19.2%. This shows a business which is only marginally profitable. Indeed a 19.2% rate of return in a high-risk business such as transportation would not make tanker business worthwhile. This is especially so given the existence of other 'no-risk' investment options such as Government treasury bills which are currently yielding returns of about 16%.

Table 7.8. **Scenario 3. Return on capital employed – ROCE (without financial charges)**

Assumptions
a) Cost of tanker – ¢150 million for a 3,000-gallon tank
b) Four working days per week

A. Operating Costs		
Item	Cost/month	Annual
Water @¢80,000 per trip for two trips/day	2,560,000	30,720,000
Fuel @¢80,000/trip	2,560,000	30,720,000
Driver's salary @¢700,000/month	700,000	8,400,000
Allowance @¢20,000/day	320,000	3,840,000
Tax	83,333	1,000,000
A1. Repairs, maintenance and replacement		
Item	Cost/month	Annual
Repairs and maintenance	1,500,000	18,000,000
Tyres replaced every year		21,000,000
A2. Total operating cost		113,680,000
A3. Depreciation		
Annual depreciation (over five years)	2,500,000	30,000,000
B. Total Cost		143,680,000
C. Revenue		
Water sales – two trips/day @¢450,000	14,400,000	172,800,000
D. Total Profit/(Loss)		29,120,000

ROCE   = $\dfrac{\text{Net Profit} \times 100}{\text{Opening Capital}}$

             = $\dfrac{29{,}120{,}000 \times 100}{150{,}000{,}000}$

             = **19.4 %**

At this rate of returns it is obvious that the business is only marginally profitable (or better still, relatively unprofitable given the high risks) even though no financial charges are involved.

Table 7.9. Scenario 4. Return on capital employed – ROCE (with financial charges)

Assumptions
a) Cost of tanker – ¢150 million for a 3,000-gallon tank
b) Four working days per week

A. Operating Costs		
Item	**Cost/month**	**Annual**
Water @¢80,000 per trip for two trips/day	2,560,000	30,720,000
Fuel @¢80,000/trip	2,560,000	30,720,000
Driver's salary @¢700,000/month	700,000	8,400,000
Allowance @¢20,000/day	320,000	3,840,000
Tax	83,333	1,000,000
Bank Interest @ 30%	3,750,000	45,000,000
A1. Repairs, maintenance and replacement		
Item	**Cost/month**	**Annual**
Repairs and maintenance	1,500,000	18,000,000
Tyres replaced every year		21,000,000
A2. Total operating cost		**158,680,000**
A3. Depreciation		
Annual depreciation (over five years)	2,500,000	30,000,000
B. Total Cost		**188,680,000**
C. Revenue		
Water sales – two trips/day @¢450,000		172,800,000
D. Total Profit/(Loss)	14,400,000	**-15,880,000**

ROCE $= \dfrac{15,880,000 \times 100}{150,000,000}$

               $= \dfrac{15.88 \times 100}{150}$

               $=$ **-10.6 %**

This scenario gives a straight negative rate of return.

Associations affiliated to the TUC through the GPRTU

The tanker associations are affiliated to the Trades Union Congress (TUC) through the Ghana Private Road Transport Union (GPRTU). This implies a formalization of the associations and their activities. This could facilitate access to certain opportunities such as credit, training and recognition.

Operations

Viable and reliable market, and high demand

The communities present a huge market for the tankers as there are large areas that are unreliably served, underserved or unserved. The reforms in the water sector still recognize that the demand gap cannot be closed in the short term, and that SWEs will play an important role in the short to medium term (MoWH). SWEs will therefore continue to experience high demand for their services, and do not see reforms as a threat to their business.

Recognized filling points created by utility

The utility has provided filling points for the tanker association members, recognizing the role that they are playing. The hydrant point has also been installed in a way that expedites filling operations.

Recognized rules for filling tanks established and followed

Tanker associations have established rules at the filling sites, which guide their members and ensure order at the filling points.

Established informal networks from supplier to the consumer

The tanker drivers have established their own network of clients, often consisting of people of different income levels and activities. A typical network consists of direct household consumers (often in high-income areas), water vendors in low-income areas, and commercial activities including food processing, laundries and construction activities. The network ensures that a tanker has a customer to serve each day.

Indicative water price to consumers established by the utility

The utility, in its agreement with the tanker associations, recommends prices which take into consideration distances covered by the drivers. The tanker drivers are supposed to stick to these prices, which are calculated using an agreed formula between the utility and the association. It was obvious from the investigation that in many cases the recommended price does not prevail, nevertheless the deviation is not much and it serves more as a guide for bargaining.

Financial

Reliable and regular earnings

The demand for SWE services creates regular and reliable earnings as consumers strive to pay their bills on time so as to be assured of regular service. In some of the high-income areas payment is made before the water is provided and many customers settle their bills promptly.

Bargain for higher prices in obvious high-demand periods

The tankers have a marketing system whereby during the dry season they bargain for higher prices from vendors and customers in high-income areas. This seasonal price differentiation allows them to cover any reduced earnings during the rainy season and from poor communities.

Trucks could be obtained on credit and paid in instalments

The major capital purchase for the tankers' business is the main tanker chassis and engine. This is expensive and could cost up to ¢100 million. Ordinarily, it would be very difficult for many of the tanker operators to save this amount, but some of the truck dealers allow buyers to pay in instalments over a period. This arrangement has greatly helped in the acquisition of tanker trucks. It is suggested that the ability of the tanker association to honour this instalment arrangement could be a strong incentive to many financial institutions.

Trucks could be hired from other operators

There is potential for vehicle owners to hire out their trucks to operators if the latter already have an established business or existing orders to supply water to customers. Therefore investors who may not necessarily want to be operators could invest in tankers.

Operators do not hire their tankers to others on days when they are not allowed to collect and deliver water.

7.10 Constraints of tanker operations

Tanker operators also face the following constraints.

Capacity and capability

Low formal education of members and leaders affects ability to negotiate

Analysis of the baseline data indicates that many of the tanker operators and even their leaders do not have much formal education. It must be recognized that some of the members have very high levels of technical education and experience, but not in management or leadership. Such training is not included in the general education curriculum, and many tanker operators found employment instead of continuing with formal education. This lack of formal education affects associations' ability to negotiate and even advocate. Opportunities for training may also be limited, as operators do not have the basics to qualify for admission to training and education programmes. What makes the situation worse is that in more than 50 per cent of cases the drivers are the real operators while the owners are involved in other businesses. The owners have little interest in the details of the business, and do not have intimate knowledge of the business.

Limited managerial capability of members

The operator's lack of education underlies their inability to keep good records, negotiate, access credit, and expand their businesses. In many cases the business is thus operated as a matter of routine, without any keen innovation and expansion.

Operations

Vehicles are old and break down often

The survey revealed that the average tanker truck is 20 years old. This leads to high maintenance costs, potentially high levels of water contamination, and unreliability in terms of response to clients. The high cost of operating the tanker is inevitably passed on to the poor household consumer.

Limited formal relationship between tankers and GWC/PURC

The tanker associations have a very limited relationship with the GWC and PURC. The relationship is limited to the provision of metered hydrant points and the setting of prices between the utility and the Association. They are not involved in any strategic planning to serve their numerous customers. The GWC's perception of the tanker association is that it is a business cartel taking advantage of a gap in supply to make a profit. The service the Association gives to its customers is not appreciated by the GWC or PURC. The PURC is now establishing a formal relationship with the tanker associations, and has already had meetings with their executives.

Source of water controlled by GWC

The water supply and hydrant sources are owned by the GWC. They determine the amount of water available to the tankers, which days the hydrants will be open, and the pressure at which it is delivered (and hence the time it takes to fill each tank). In the case of the Lashibi Tanker Association, for instance, the tankers could only fill up on four days a week. In some cases they are unable to fill up at all. This makes the business very uncertain and unpredictable, relying on the 'benevolence' of the GWC.

No regulatory system for checking quality of water and price to consumers

The tanker associations do not have any means of checking the quality of the water being sold from tankers, nor is there any independent means of checking. With this uncertainty customers sometimes suspect the quality of the water (see Box 11.1). The same situation affects price to consumers, as there is no means of checking whether the recommended prices are applied.

Tankers as excuse for inability to supply certain areas

Tanker operators have in many ways become an easy excuse for water shortages in certain areas of Accra. This has often resulted in disconnections of filling points, the most visible being the disconnections in Teshie (Acolor, 2001) and Lashibi (in April, 2004).[20] This line of action has often been taken by the utility in response to pressure from already served customers or from politicians. In some areas the very consumers served by the tankers accuse them of being the cause of the dry pipes. Some consumers in areas which are not served at all think the tankers have colluded with the utility to not extend services to their area. During the dry season when there is a high demand for water a tanker business should be thriving, but it is during this period that some customers become resentful.

Financial

High investment capital

The tanker business requires very high investment capital, currently at least ¢110 million per truck. This covers the head of a 20-year-old truck and a locally constructed tank (a new truck would cost about ¢500 million according to the chairman of the Private Water Tanker Owners' Association). As few of the operators can secure credit, the challenge is great. It is little wonder that most tanker drivers do not own their trucks, but operate on behalf of those with more money.

High operational expenses due to age of vehicles

The operational expenses of the trucks are very high because they are so old – our assessment shows that running costs are about six times that of a new truck. The poor state of the roads, especially in the new and informal settlements, partly accounts for the frequent breakdown of the vehicles.

No reliable financial records

The tanker operators do not keep reliable financial records. During the field survey many operators saw the keeping of financial records as tedious and a waste of time.

---

15. It must be noted that water supplied for construction activities is often collected from nearby ponds and not from the utility. This raises serious concerns for water quality. One association confirmed that some tankers do carry raw water to construction sites, thus compromising the quality of water purchased from GWC (as the next tanker load may be contaminated by polluted residue). However their members have been told not to do this, even though it is difficult to police the practice. This practice may also affect concrete quality for construction projects.

16. In deciding on the freight element of tanker-delivered water, reference is made to the guidelines used by the state institution responsible for the determination of national freight rates.

17. From discussions with the Chief Executive of the Labour Enterprise Trust, 20th May 2004.

18. Two coping strategies could emerge from this current arrangement. The first is that tankers go to places further away to collect water for their customers on the days they cannot collect from their regular filling point, and then charge substantially above the 'normal' rate. The second, which is not admitted by the Association, is that some tanker drivers may in fact use the truck to fetch raw water to serve construction sites, with serious implications for water quality.

19. One tanker operator, who at one point owned five tankers, now has only one and indicated that he has moved into the hospitality business because of the low returns in the water business.

20. In April, 2004 following a series of television reports on frequent water shortages at Sakumono, a middle-class estate near Lashibi, the GWC disconnected the filling point serving the Lashibi Tankers' Association. This led to a doubling of the rates charged to consumers dependent on their services, as they had to collect water from much further away. Following persistent counter outcry from the Association and a series of meetings with the utility, their activities were reduced to four days a week instead of the previous six days. Current rates are yet to reflect this new development.

Chapter 8

Small Water Enterprises (vendors)

8.1 Vendors – historical perspective

Vendors, as described earlier, are located in communities that are unserved or underserved. They form the second link in the supply chain. Unlike the tanker operators, vendors still operate as individuals and many attempts to organize them have failed. Water vending is an old practice that was being carried out long before independence in 1957. Water was collected in 20-litre containers from public standpipes (free at the time) and carried to households two at a time, using a pole across the carrier's shoulders. A lot of Fulani migrants to Accra and other cities and towns specialized in this trade, and were popularly known as kaya. When public standpipes were withdrawn in favour of domestic connections this business shifted to the sale of water to neighbours from the domestic tap.[21] In areas that were not served, the tankers that had been delivering water for construction purposes converted to carting water for vendors in unserved areas. With more vendors establishing themselves, especially in informal low-income communities, the demand for water through domestic vendors increased.

8.2 Accommodation status of vendors

A typical vendor lives in a family house shared with eight other households. As shown in Figure 8.1, 30 per cent of the vendors interviewed are tenants. The tenants require the permission of landlords to construct an underground storage facility; therefore many of the tenants use polythene containers, which can be moved easily when one has to relocate. Water vending is generally a woman's job, reinforcing the long association of women with water supply in Ghana.

The few men involved in water vending are landlords or pensioners who engage in the trade to supplement their income. In addition to selling water, women usually sell other household items on small tables and in kiosks.

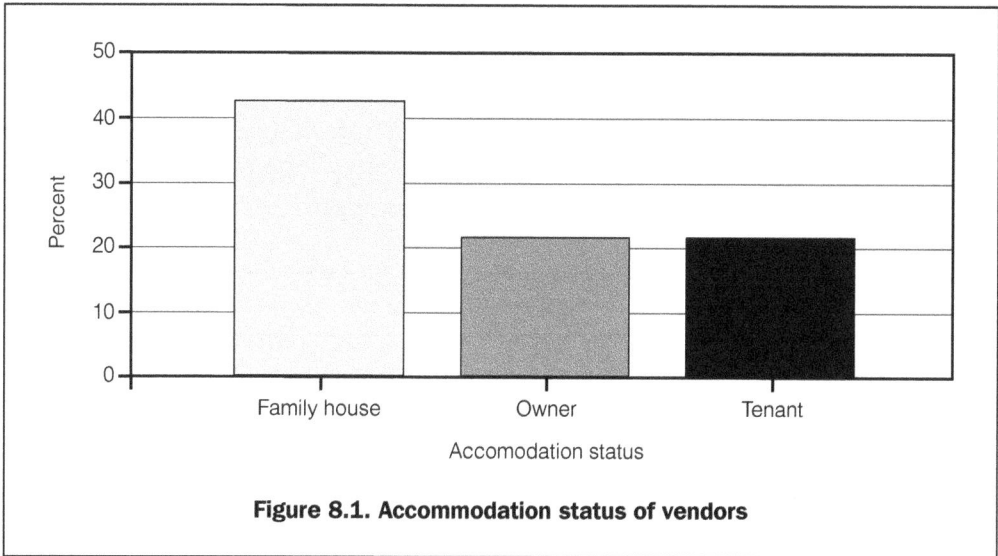

Figure 8.1. Accommodation status of vendors

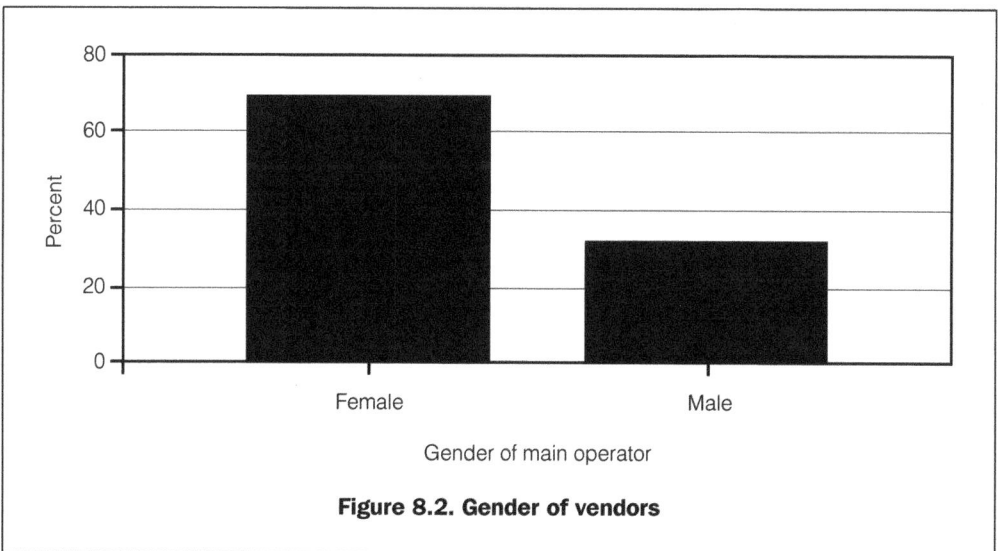

Figure 8.2. Gender of vendors

8.3 Capital acquisition

A typical water vending business involves acquiring a water storage facility of between 1,000 gallons (4,500 litres) and 4,500 gallons. In a number of cases the storage facilities were built underground, but in recent years the use of polythene containers has become more popular. It costs about ¢2.5million to build a 3,000-gallon underground storage tank.

The cost of polythene storage tanks range from ¢3 million to ¢10 million. For many low-income households this is impossible. Of those who have purchased tanks, however, only about 32 per cent acquired a loan for the purpose while nearly 28 per cent mobilized the money themselves. Many others also depend on plough-back from other businesses as well as lump-sum payments (from a husband, for example) enabling them to set up in business. The most interesting aspect is that the investment in the business is mobilized over a very long period and the items are acquired as and when the capital becomes available.

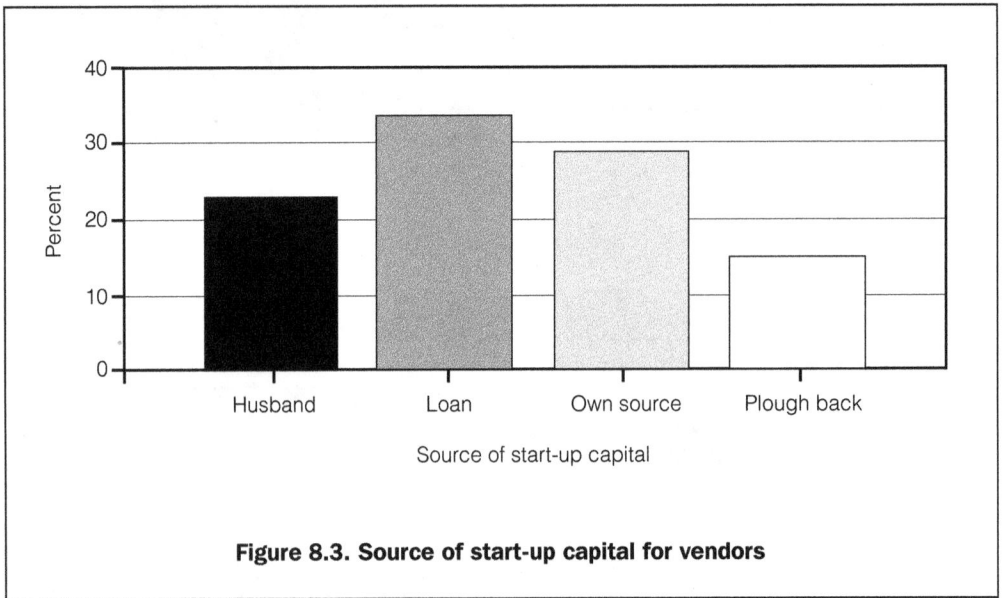

Figure 8.3. Source of start-up capital for vendors

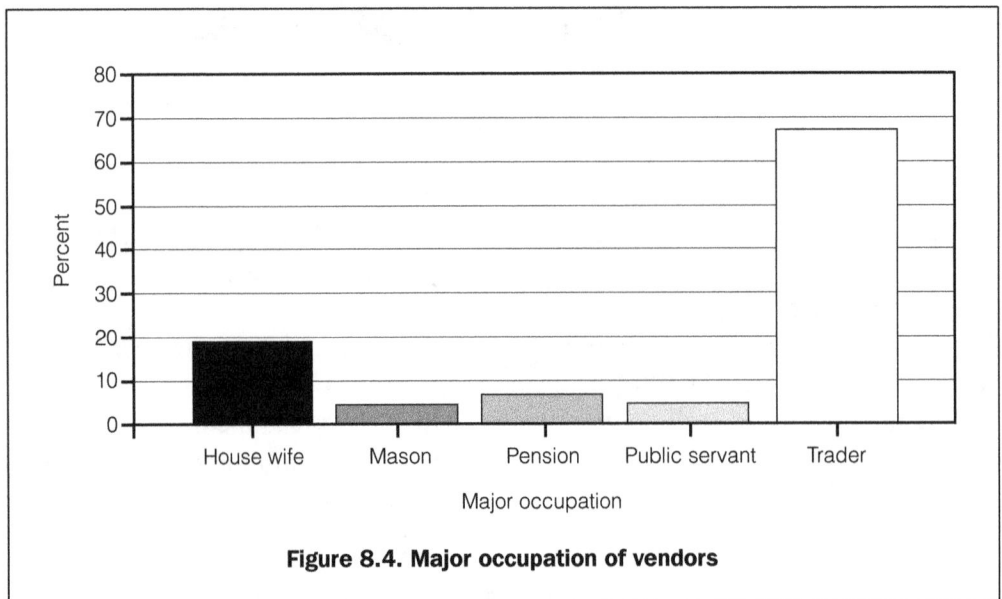

Figure 8.4. Major occupation of vendors

Some of the vendors are engaged in other activities and selling water is only one of many sources of livelihood for the low-income household. Nearly 70 per cent of those interviewed are traders, while a significant 20 per cent are housewives. For those who are traders more than 50 per cent of their trading income is from water vending.

8.4   Accessing water to sell

The demand for water is so great that vendors are more concerned about getting enough water to sell, rather than marketing their product to find new customers. The main source of water for 95 per cent of vendors is tankers.

There are a few vendors who are in served areas who also secure water from the GWC mains. It must be noted that since vending water from the GWC mains is illegal (according to the GWC), a lot of the vendors did not disclose this source. It was observed that in some areas the water may only flow once a week and many of the vendors fill their storage facilities and then rely on the tankers when this source is exhausted.

Although many of the vendors are customers of specific tanker operators, some of them go to the filling point to make sure that the operators respond to their request. The vendors said that during the dry seasons securing water from the tanker operators becomes very difficult and one may have to wait at the filling point for more than a day just to secure one tanker load of water. This is because of the competition from water-sachet producers and contractors who need the water for construction purposes.

At the vendor's home the water is stored in either purpose-built underground tanks or polythene containers of different sizes. Some 10 per cent of vendors interviewed supplement the underground tanks with polythene containers (see Figure 8.6). The storage facility is the major capital asset of many vendors, and many keep adding to their capacity as the business expands.

Vendor's storage capacity ranged from 1000 to 6500 gallons (see Figure 8.7). Even so, 60 per cent of vendors claim that their storage capacity is inadequate, especially during the dry season when demand is very high.

8.5   Pricing and competition

Vendors price their water according to several factors, the key ones being the price they paid for the water, the demand for water in the neighbourhood, the quality of water, and the identity of the buyer. Tanker operators generally sell water to the vendors at about ¢33/litre (see Table 6.3, which shows water costing ¢55,000/m³ and a total of 60% of this going to the tanker operator and utility). So for a vendor

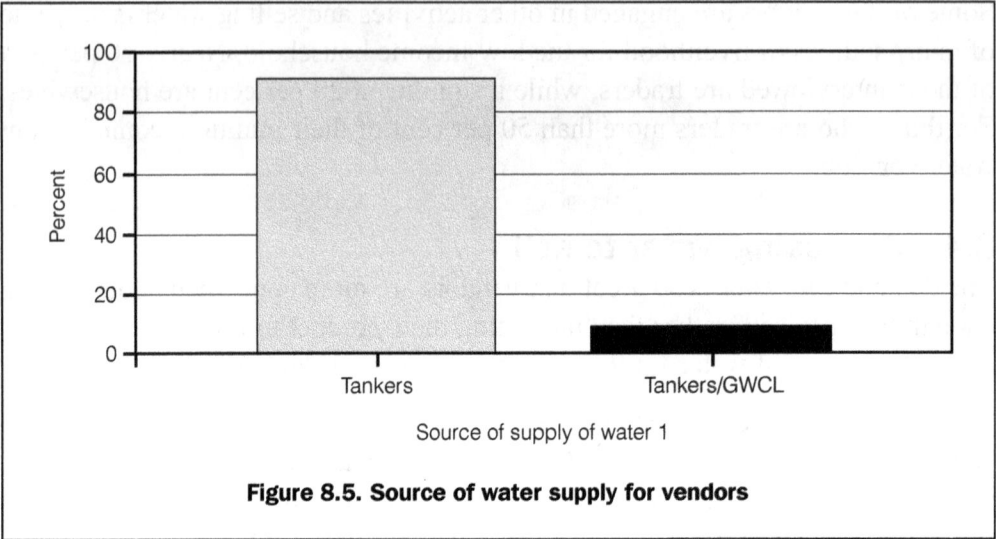

Figure 8.5. Source of water supply for vendors

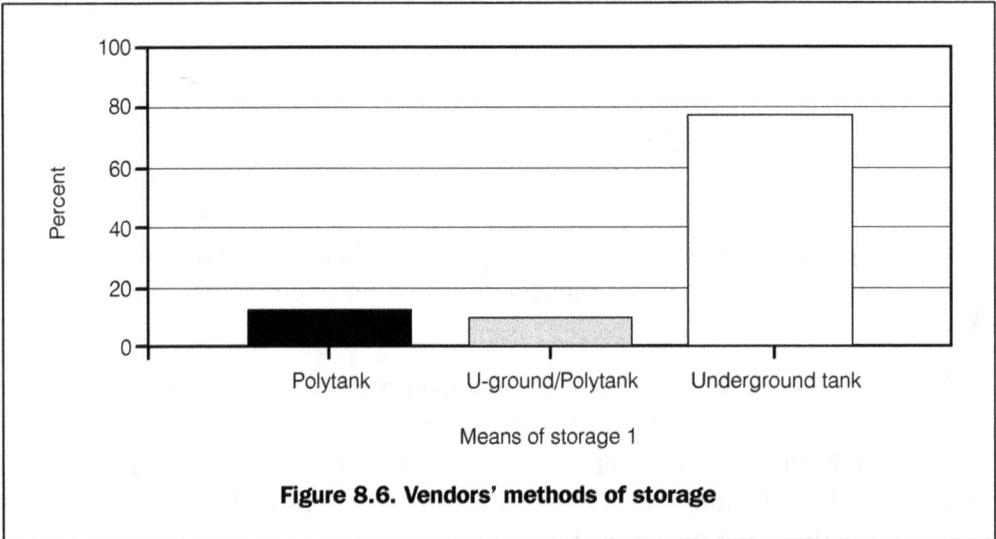

Figure 8.6. Vendors' methods of storage

to cover their costs they have to sell above ¢594 per 18-litre bucket, and usually charge in the range of ¢700-¢1000 (¢39-56/litre). This implies that the vendor's profit margin, without taking any other costs into consideration, will be between 18 and 70 per cent. It looks, on the face of it, a lucrative and viable business.[22]

Vendors believe they are facing more competition as more people are joining the business. It is now easier to acquire storage – polythene tanks – and some stores even sell them on credit. The demand on the tankers has thus gone up, though they work for only four days a week. It is ironic that while the market is increasing access to water is decreasing. The main competition is for water, and not the market.

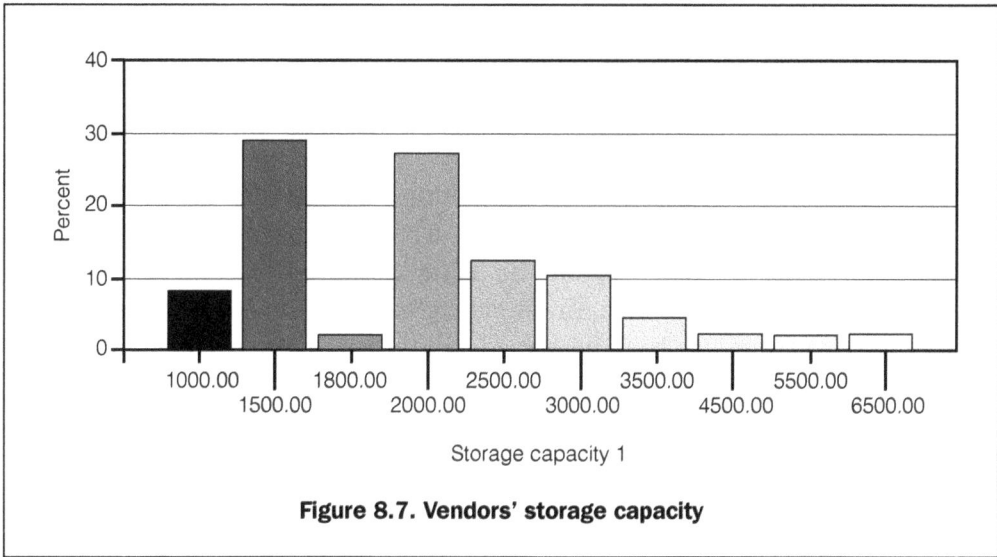

Figure 8.7. Vendors' storage capacity

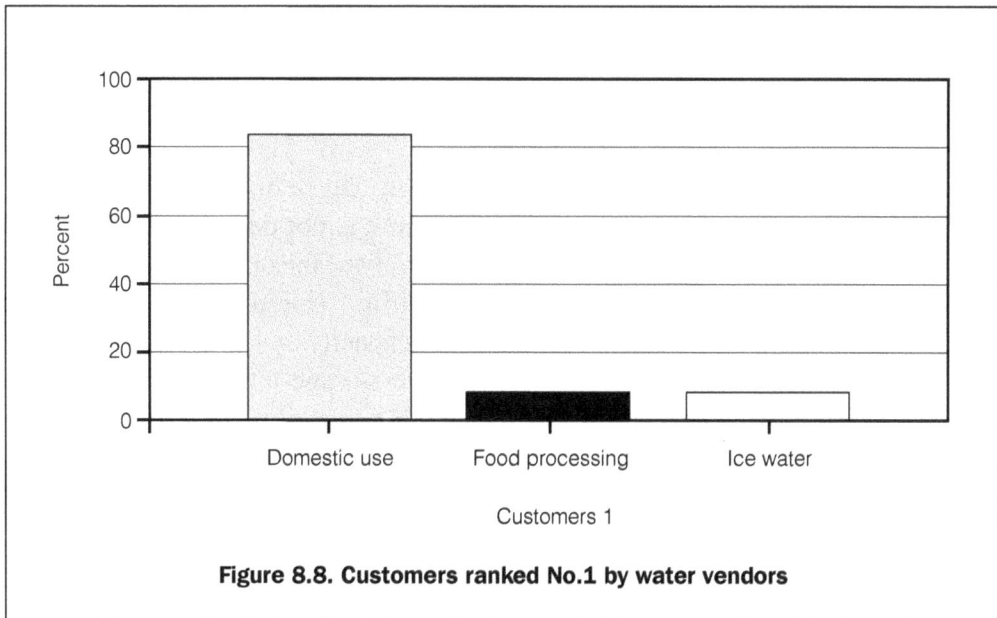

Figure 8.8. Customers ranked No.1 by water vendors

8.6 Reaching the consumers

Vendors have three major customers: (a) direct household users (for domestic activities), (b) food processors, and (c) iced-water sellers. The prime clients are the domestic users who account for 80 per cent of sales. Although they buy less, vendors ranked food processors and iced-water sellers as being as important as their domestic use customers, with no 'second rank' customers.

8.7 Viability of water vending

Assessing vendors' financial situation has been very difficult. This is because they use the water that they buy for their own domestic uses, as well as selling it, and do not keep separate records. Viability could only be assessed through estimation.

The assessment of the vendors' financial position is based upon the two periods of the dry season and the wet season. In the dry season the demand for water is very high and the price responds accordingly, while in the wet season, the demand is relatively low, and so is the price. In estimating the viability of vendor operations the following assumptions have been made, based on findings from the survey:

Dry season	Wet season	Storage facility
Water is sold at ¢800 per bucket and 4000 gals (1000 buckets) are sold daily	Water is sold at ¢600 per bucket and 667 gals (167 buckets) are sold daily	Cost is assumed to be recouped in two years
Labour cost (selling, cleaning) is ¢60,000 daily	Labour cost for selling and cleaning is assumed to be ¢30,000 daily	

The analysis indicates the following:

During the dry season as much as ¢2.88 million can be made per month (see Table 8.1). When depreciation for the storage tank is not deducted, this rises to ¢3.36 million per month. On the other hand viability of the operations is marginal during the wet season, dropping to ¢0.18 million (including deduction for depreciation). Annually a vendor with a storage capacity of 4,000 gallons (18 m³) will make ¢19.4 million (if depreciation for the storage tank is not deducted), indicating a 16.5 per cent on turnover. This, on the face of it, appears a lucrative business.

This figure can be adjusted to reflect the consumption of the vendor's household, assuming a total of 240 litres for the household per day. This brings their annual consumption to ¢3.36 million, which represents money that will not be available for their use in the business. However since they are not going to budget for expenditure on water, the household's disposable income will be higher.

One water vendor said at the workshop that she makes on average '¢50,000' of profit a day, on a very good day in the dry season, on a tank capacity of 3000 gallons. This is gross earnings. A reasonable portion of the available water, which is not accounted for, goes into household consumption and shortfalls on tanker deliveries.

Vendors rarely cost their time into the management of the businesses.

Table 8.1. Assessment of viability of vendor operations

Income assessment (Dry season)			Expenditure assessment			
Amount of water sold	Amount in gallons	Amount earned (¢)	Water purchased (¢)	Labour	Storage facility	Total
Per day	4000	800,000	600,000	60,000	20,000	680,000
Per week	24000	4,800,000	3,600,000	360,000	120,000	4,080,000
Per month	96000	19,200,000	14,400,000	1,440,000	480,000	16,320,000
Per six months dry season	576000	115,200,000	86,400,000	8,640,000	2,880,000	97,920,000
Profit (six months)		17,280,000				
Earnings per month		2,880,000				
Income assessment (wet season)			**Expenditure assessment**			
Per day	667	100,050	75,000	30,000	20,000	125,000
Per week	4002	600,300	450,000	180,000	120,000	750,000
Per month	16008	2,401,200	1,800,000	720,000	480,000	3,000,000
Per six month wet season	96048	14,407,200	10,800,000	4,320,000	2,880,000	18,000,000
Profit (Loss) for six months		**-3,592,800**				
Earnings per month		**-299,400**				

Total annual earnings (Annual)   13,687,200
Add back depreciation on storage facility   5,760,000
Total cash earnings (Annual)   **19,447,200**

Opportunities for vendors

Average time in operation
Vendors have been in the business on average for five years. The survey encountered one person who has been in the business for over 25 years. Many of the vendors have accumulated business experience that could enable them to be stable enough to anticipate risks and manage them.

Water vending as an additional source of income
Many of the water vendors sell other items too. Some have kiosks where they sell other household items. These complementary activities provide additional income.

Established markets and customers
Many of the vendors have established customers with a regular demand. It is thus very easy for a vendor to assess the market to meet any excess or shortage. Individual arrangements can be made with customers to meet their payments over a week or month. The iced-water sellers buy in the morning and pay at the end of each day.

Established supply sources
For those vendors who rely on GWC sources the flow is unpredictable, but for those who rely on tankers the supply is quite reliable, and in hard times the vendors go to the hydrant filling point so that they can trail the tanker operator.

Non-competitive pricing
Pricing is relatively non-competitive as the vendors establish the price informally. The basic price is dependent on what price the tanker operator is charging. Those who sell GWC water directly to neighbours have a mark-up of around 50 per cent.

Constraints

No formal recognition by the GWC or PURC
The vendors, unlike the tankers, have no formal recognition from the GWC and are often considered either as domestic users or commercial clients and rates are fixed accordingly for those connected to GWC mains. Vendors served only by tanker have no relationship with the GWC or PURC. The GWC says that vendors using their supply are illegal, as in some cases they prevent other users from getting supplies by using suction pumps to draw water from the mains. Their business is therefore under threat, and they could face disconnection at anytime.[23]

No means of assessing the quality of water

There is no way of assessing the quality of water delivered by the tanker or the GWC mains, nor after it has been stored in the vendor's tanks. The vendors claim they smell, taste and check for colour as a means of assessing the quality. There is a big risk to the end-user, who uses the water on trust.

Limited education

Few vendors have much formal education and therefore record keeping is virtually non-existent. Because income from other trading is mixed with income from water and records are not kept of the vendor's own domestic use, they are not able to tell exactly how much they earn from their vending activities.

---

21. In the early 1980s the GWC decided to discontinue the use of public standpipes in the major cities and to shift demand to house connections due to a number of factors, including the difficulty of managing the standpipes (personal communication, Chief Manager, ATMA Accra East).

22. A vendor's costs will include amortization of the capital cost of the storage facility, salary/wages for the attendant, cleaning, and disinfection. Most vendors do not 'pay' themselves and do not see this as a cost.

23. During the interview with the Chief Manager (Accra East) he indicated that his office would soon go round to disconnect all vendors whose activities were affecting the flow of water to other residents.

Chapter 9

Consumer Perspectives
on Small Water Enterprises

9.1 Introduction – Consumer types and categories

There are three major types of water consumers identified during this study: (a) consumers in the informal low-income communities who use water mainly for domestic chores; (b) food processors who are mainly kenkey producers,[24] street-food sellers and small restaurants; and (c) iced-water sellers who buy water, keep it in the fridge and sell in quantities of about a pint each in kiosks, in the markets and on the street.

9.2 Uses of water

The figures below show the ranking of different uses of water by consumers.

The use of purchased water determines the amount purchased, the price consumers are willing to pay, and even the quality. The field survey revealed that 38 per cent of consumers purchase water mainly for domestic cooking. This is followed by a

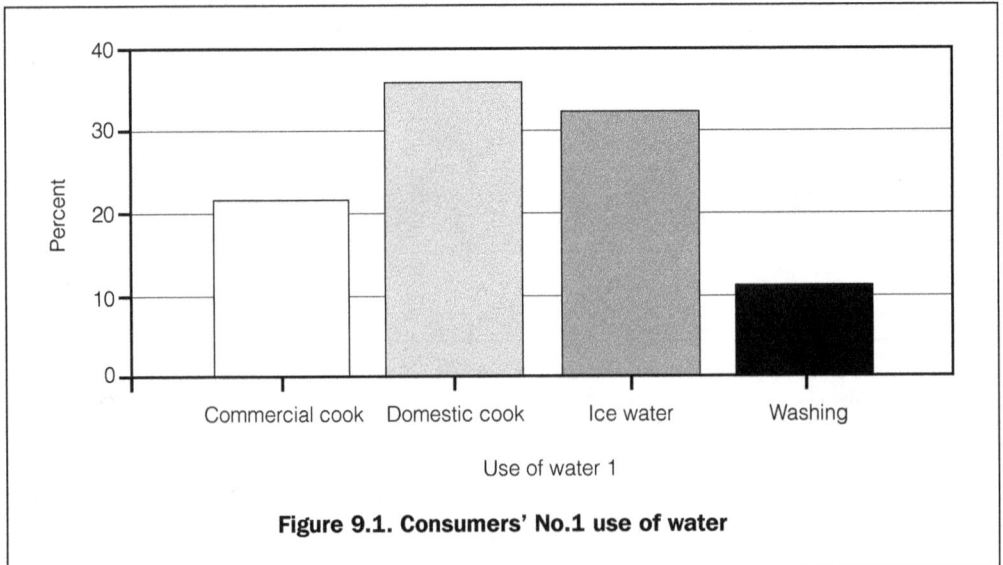

Figure 9.1. Consumers' No.1 use of water

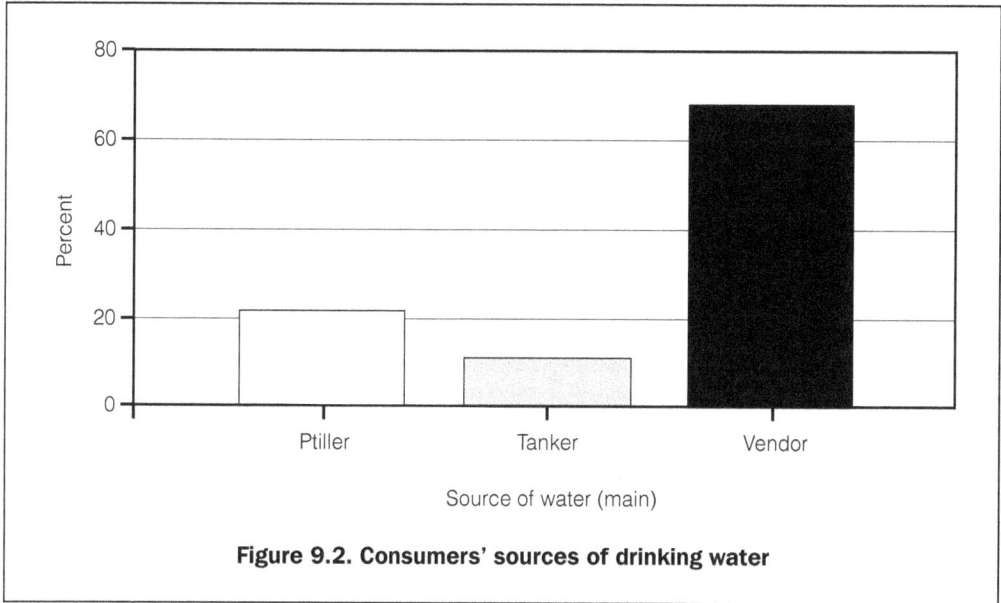

Figure 9.2. Consumers' sources of drinking water

surprising 32 per cent that purchase water for re-packaging, freezing and selling. A further 22 per cent purchase water for preparing commercial food, while the last 10 per cent use it for domestic washing. For secondary use of water domestic washing made up 50 per cent while the rest was for domestic and commercial cooking. The high domestic use of water indicates that consumers would be much more concerned with water quality and price as these directly affect them.

The high use of water for iced-water selling indicates that many water consumers are themselves sellers. Many such consumers thus have a dual interest when it comes to pricing and access. The inability to secure water will not only affect domestic activities but will also affect their livelihood. This means that their supply must be very reliable and the price very competitive.

9.3 Choice of supply options

SWEs are a crucial source of drinking water for many consumers in the low-income unserved communities where the case studies were carried out. The three key sources were from water vendors, directly from tanker operators, and from motorized carts.

The interviews revealed that about 68 per cent of those surveyed depend on vendors as their first source of water supply. Second-most important are the motorized carts, accounting for 20 per cent of consumers, while the remaining 12 per cent depend on direct tanker services.

9.4 Cost of water

The cost of water is crucial to consumers and from their perspective it is the greatest worry.

The range of prices for 10 litres of water is shown in Figure 9.3. The price ranges from ¢360 to ¢500, with 33 per cent of consumers buying the water at ¢400. The price differences are accounted for by both the source of water and the quantity purchased.

Figure 9.4 presents the end-user price differences by different sources. Interestingly, the difference between a consumer of water from the GWC mains and one who uses a vendor who depends on a tanker operator is about 200 per cent. While the privileged low-income consumer pays ¢18/litre, the vendor-dependent consumer – in addition to all the inconvenience – pays ¢55.5/litre. GWC has recommended that tanker operators charge ¢23.7/litre, but they usually charge ¢33.3/litre. The exception is Labour Enterprises Trust tankers, who charge ¢27.7/litre.

It is obvious that consumers who buy water from vendors are paying exorbitant rates. Unfortunately these are often poor people living in unserved informal settlements. The concern is how these poor households manage to afford these high rates. Some do take advantage of credit arrangements when offered (see Figure 9.5).

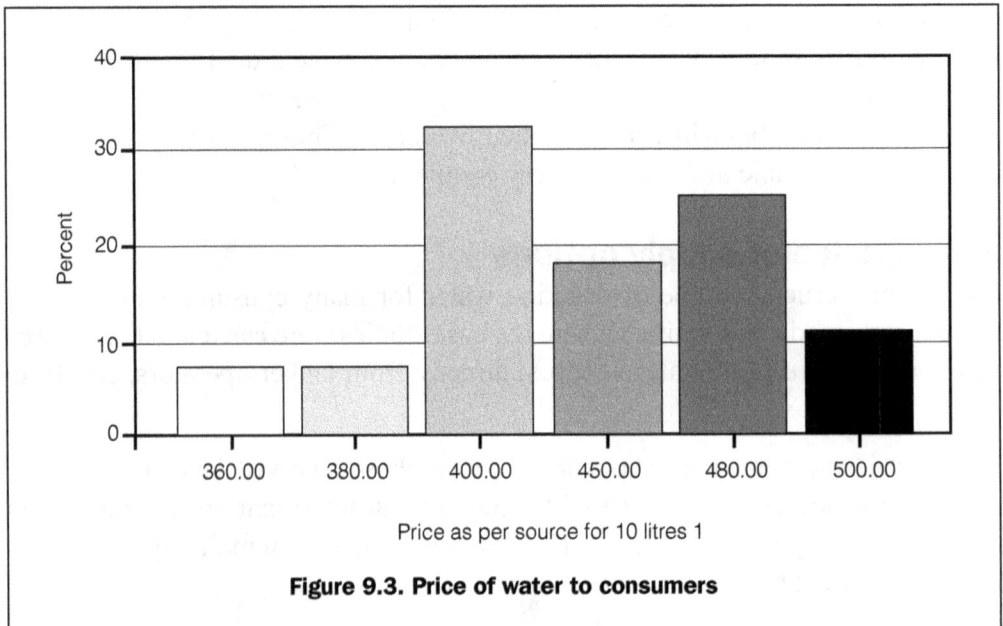

Figure 9.3. Price of water to consumers

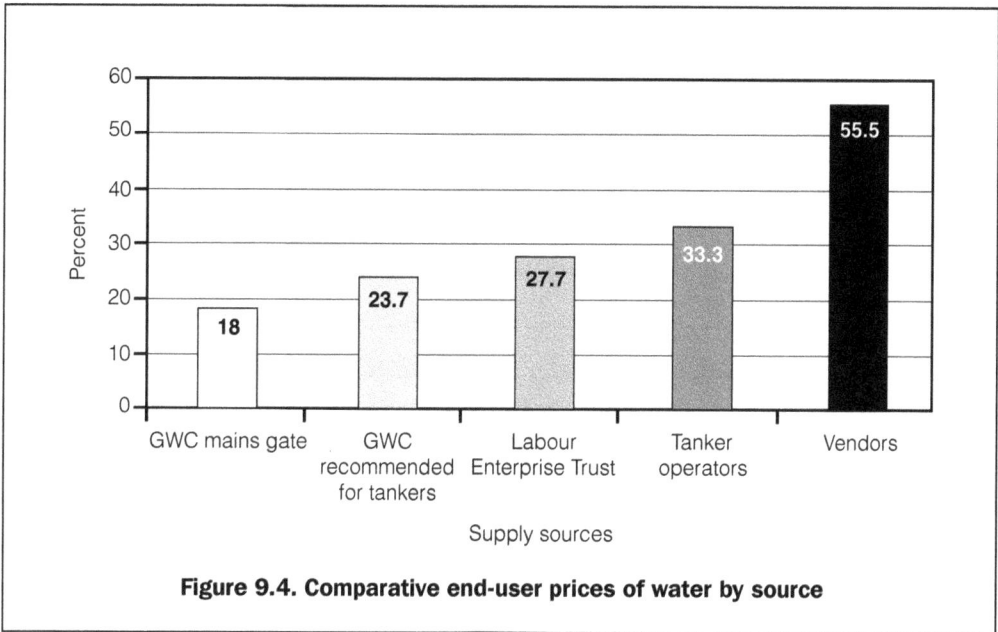

Figure 9.4. Comparative end-user prices of water by source

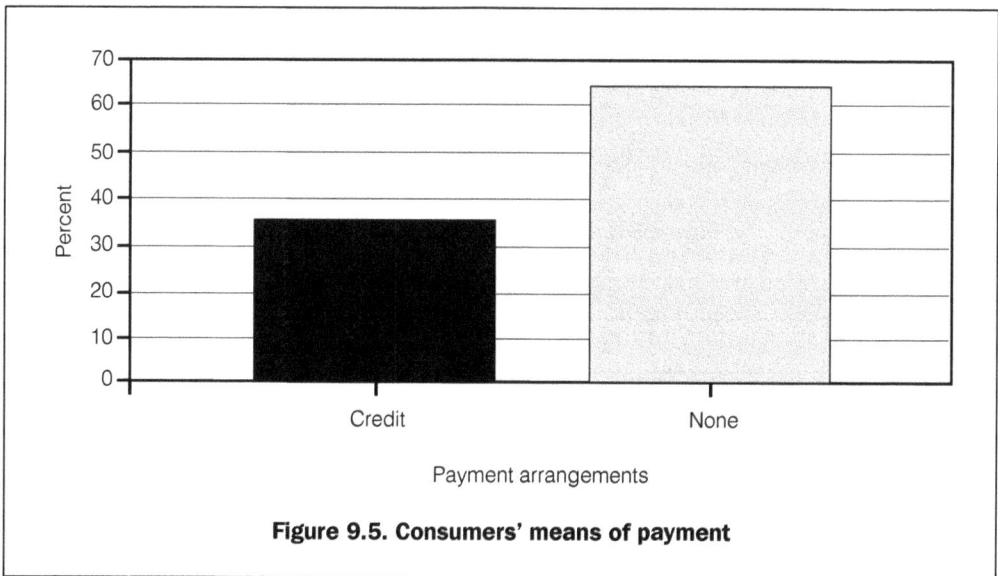

Figure 9.5. Consumers' means of payment

Figure 9.5 shows that 37 per cent of poor people buy water on credit and settle as soon as they can. Trust is vital in sustaining this option. In 63 per cent of cases people prefer to pay up front rather than carry a debt for water. This is in sharp contrast to supply from GWC where bills are settled on a monthly basis.

Poor consumers also purchase water only in the quantities that they can use at one time, often in 18-litre buckets. Few have domestic storage except for aluminium barrels and buckets. While 35 per cent of poor households use buckets to store water, 32 per cent use barrels and the remaining 33 per cent have no storage and purchase directly for use (see Figure 9.6). Neither the buckets nor the barrels have covers, thus compromising the quality of the water.

Consumers key areas of concern with their current water supply arrangements are pricing and quality of water. Consumers are only too aware of the problems created by pricing in an under-supplied market. In a neo-liberal political atmosphere

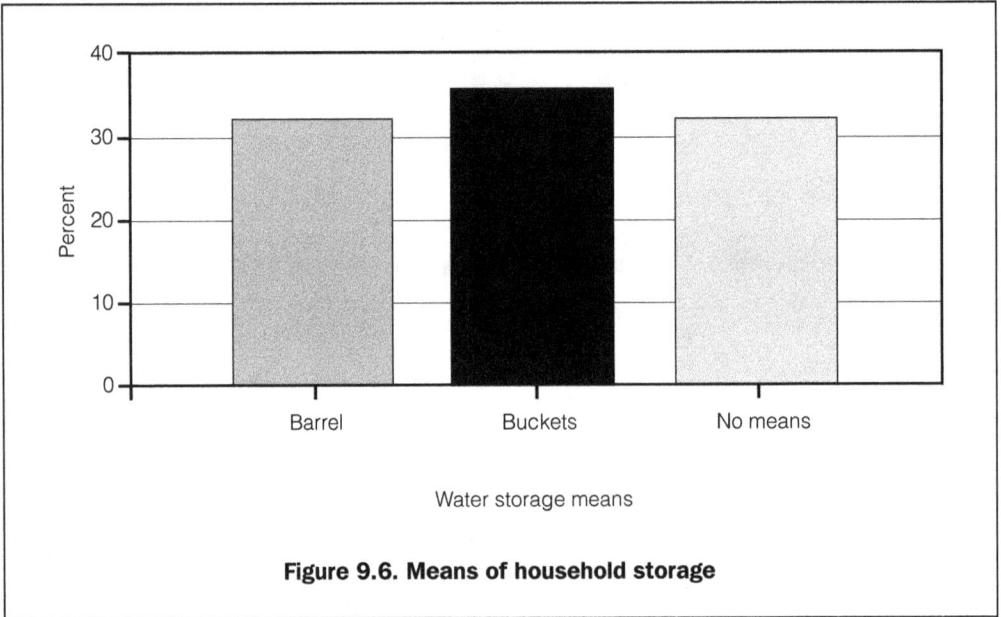

Figure 9.6. Means of household storage

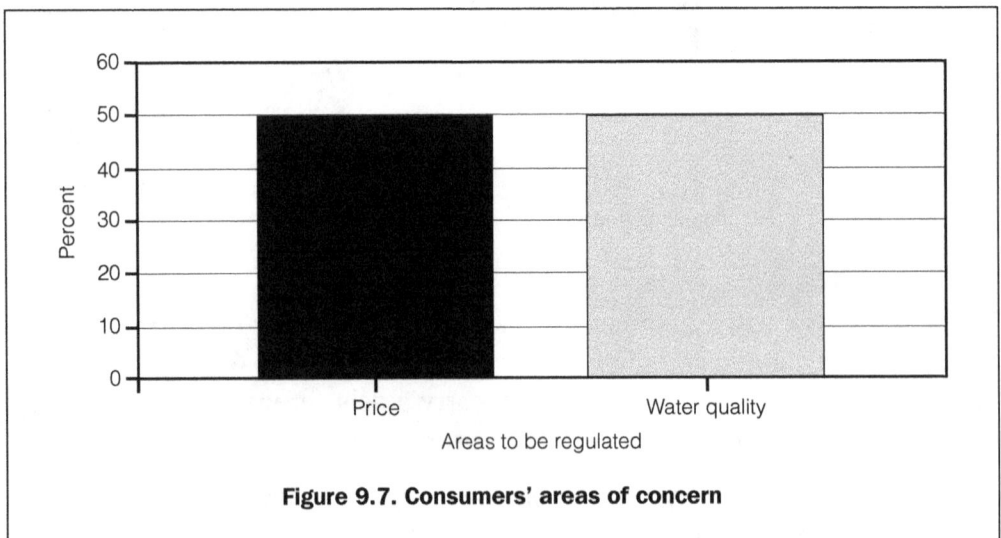

Figure 9.7. Consumers' areas of concern

where there is virtually no alternative free or subsidized access, the pain of high charges falls on the consumer and particularly on poor households with no mains connection.

9.5   Water quality

For the consumer, water quality is crucial as the cost of healthcare is often far higher than high-quality water. Unfortunately, neither the suppliers nor the consumers have any means of assessing water quality. The system thus operates on trust and neighbourliness. Consumers in very doubtful situations have applied only one major means of testing quality, which is the colour of the water. Although colour is indeed one way of assessing water quality, that alone is not enough to judge the wholesomeness of water. The responsibility for checking water quality lies with the Food and Drugs Board (FDB) and the PURC. For many consumers water quality is the most uncertain aspect of the water transporting operation. The organization of the tankers into Associations has brought about some regulation and responsibility, but not for the numerous vendors operating in the neighbourhoods whose underground tank may be just 20 metres from a latrine or major drain. It is also difficult to clean underground tanks, an issue that came out during the workshop.

Opportunities for consumers

SWEs are the most reliable water providers for poor communities
According to consumers SWEs are the most reliable water providers and are more regular than the GWC mains. If you have a business that uses water, again SWEs are the most dependable suppliers.

Obtaining water on credit
One of the key advantages of SWEs – and a key coping strategy – is that some vendors and tankers will supply on credit. Households can therefore get water when they have no money, and they can also buy only what they need or can afford.

Help in preserving water and cost
In principle households pay for their water as they buy it. This harsh reality means that people use water efficiently to reduce their costs. With a monthly billing system one can neither bargain nor pay in instalments.

Constraints

Price hikes during high demand periods
The major constraint in relying on vendors is that prices go up during the dry

season and periods of serious shortages – and this in a supply situation that is already burdensome for poor consumers. The price per bucket increased from ¢800 to ¢1,200 in just a day when the GWC did not allow the tankers at Lashibi to fill for a day in April 2004. The price changes happen so fast that practically every vendor changes price simultaneously.

Perceived collusion between GWC and SWEs to not extend mains
Some consumers believe that the SWEs have connived with the GWC not to supply them with water or extend the mains to the community. Others believe that because it is perceived by the government that they have access to potable water, the GWC does not initiate plans to extend the mains to the respective poor and voiceless communities. To them no one seems to appreciate the difficulties they face.

Water quality cannot be assured
One criticism of the SWEs is that there is no reliable means of assessing or maintaining water quality. Consumers are very sceptical of the water quality and buy only from trusted sources. The vendors' water is better than any other alternative where there is no mains supply.

No defined complaints point
The consumers identified as a problem that there are no established complaints procedures or points. When there is an abuse by a tanker operator or vendor, customers only point of complaint is the police, and often their complaint is not pursued.

---

24. *Kenkey* is a popular local maize preparation that is consumed by both rich and poor, and is best taken with fish.

Chapter 10

Utilities, Agencies and Reforms

10.1 GPRS/HIPC and poverty reduction initiatives

The Ghana Poverty Reduction Strategy recognizes that increasing access to potable water is key to achieving better health and sustained poverty reduction. Its strategies thus focus on improving access in rural, peri-urban and unreached poor urban areas through effective management of urban systems, safe liquid and solid waste management, and capacity building for environmental health (GoG, 2003, Vol.1). One of the core indicators in the GPRS is to 'halve, by 2015, the proportion of people without sustainable access to safe drinking water'.

Within the context of urban water systems management, the GPRS seeks to improve service delivery through the design of monitorable implementation plans for effective programming of linked activities with the GWC (as utility), private operators (including SWEs) and PURC (the regulatory body). The urban poor households' (and particularly those living in compound houses) access to water will be promoted through a reassessment of the lifeline tariff. The targets for the period 2002–04 and 2003–05 in the sector are to improve access to safe water from 70 to 78 per cent in urban areas and from 40 to 54 per cent in rural areas.[25]

10.2 Reaching the informal/poor urban consumer

The GPRS recommends a number of pro-poor water supply interventions, including:

- direct state interventions in areas where there is a marked gap in service delivery;
- partnership programmes with NGOs which have a comparative advantage in responding effectively to the needs of the vulnerable and excluded;
- promotion of physical planning in both urban and rural contexts to provide a salubrious environment for living; and
- redevelopment of urban slums, starting in old neighbourhoods with high population densities, to cover about 500,000 people by 2004.

10.3   Relationship between utilities and agencies with SWEs

At the 2002 Project Launch Workshop, it was quite clear that many people perceived SWEs as exploiters whose activities ought to be curtailed or controlled. The following sections look at the perspectives of key institutions in relation to SWEs.

Ministry of Works and Housing

Among some of the significant attempts by the Ministry of Works and Housing to address the provision of water to poor and low-income urban communities is the establishment of a unit to monitor the provision of water to low-income households in urban areas (GoG, 2003). In addition the Ministry is contemplating the establishment of a working group – provisionally known as the Urban Low-Income Group Working Unit – to work out modalities, policies and programmes for the provision of water to the urban poor. The remit of the unit includes defining equity rules for ensuring supply of water to both networked areas and communities which are currently unserved/underserved.[26]

The draft contract documents signed by the consultant for the earlier lease arrangement for the urban water sector include provisions for the involvement of tanker operators. The principal reasons are: (a) there is such a huge gap in meeting investment requirements that not all communities can be served in the very future; (b) due to the poor planning of most parts of the country's cities, especially Accra, the utility needs to work with SWEs to reach some areas in a cost-effective manner; and (c) the relatively high incidence of urban poverty and people's inability to afford house connections means that other service options are necessary. These options will in some cases have to involve SWEs.

Ghana Water Company

The evidence points to the fact that only the GWC has had a formal relationship with SWEs, notably tanker operators. This is through bilateral agreements with the tanker associations. Through the Articles of Agreement with the tankers' associations, the GWC tries to loosely regulate their operations in the areas of water quality and price (see Appendix 6). In contrast, however, our discussions with the utility's managers indicated that the activities of domestic vendors are deemed to be illegal from the perspective of the GWC. It is interesting to note, however, that whilst the GWC claims no formal relationship with domestic vendors, those who depend on water supplied by the utility are billed at a commercial rate. This obviously recognizes a contractual relationship.

Public Utilities Regulatory Commission

Neither the PURC nor any government body specifically regulates or supports the operations of SWEs at the moment. However the situation is changing as the PURC now believes that activities of secondary and tertiary providers need greater attention and support to make their operations more beneficial to the poor people they serve. The Commission has been very mindful of the fact that many low-income households in urban areas depend to a large extent on the services of secondary and tertiary suppliers for their water needs. This was confirmed by the findings of the socio-economic study they undertook in 2001/2, which established that around 60 per cent of poor people receive their water from tanker and cart operators and from vendors (including neighbour-sellers) (BiG/ASI, 2002). The PURC is developing a 'Social Policy Framework' for the provision of utility services with a view to ensuring equity and fairness. It is also taking a closer look at the operations of SWEs, particularly tankers.[27] What is now clear is that the Commission will regulate water quality but will not at the moment do so with regard to pricing.

In line with their desire to have SWEs' operations make a more positive impact on low-income households, PURC is looking at how the costs associated with the operations of secondary suppliers, particularly tankers, could be brought down and the savings passed on to the unserved. This is unlikely to be done by price regulation, but instead by, for example, asking the utility to bring hydrants/filling points closer to the users (where this is technically possible) to reduce the transport element in the cost of delivered water (which could be as high as 80 per cent). PURC has drafted some guidelines (in consultation with the GWC and the tanker associations) to ensure the quality of water supplied by tankers.

Department of Town and Country Planning

The T&CPD has never considered the case of SWEs in their design and planning of urban areas, nor the provision of utility services to informal communities. Their planning always assumes a piped network system to be provided by the public utility. For the T&CPD, the informal communities do not 'exist', as no formal provision is made for them for facilities and services. These attitudes and perceptions are changing, however, and either through silent acquiescence or through active encouragement by the public, informal settlements are being serviced either by the utility or by SWEs.

10.4 Reforms and implications

Since 1993 the Government of Ghana (GoG) has initiated reforms in the sector to enable various sector actors to play significant roles in the delivery of services, improve efficiency, and achieve financial equilibrium for the sector. Key elements of the reforms have been the decoupling of rural water from the urban water supply (1994) and establishment of the Community Water and Sanitation Agency (CWSA); the decision to implement increased private sector participation (PSP) in the management of the urban water sector (1996); and the establishment of two oversight and regulatory bodies, the Public Utilities Regulatory Commission (1997) and Water Resources Commission (1998).

By far the most radical of the measures is the introduction of PSP into urban water delivery, which involves turning the GWC into an asset-holding company and letting a private operator manage operations under a management contract for four years. The contract could roll over into a lease arrangement in its fifth year. It is expected that the procurement process and hand over to an operator will be completed by the middle of 2005. In parallel with the reforms, GoG is undertaking major capital expenditures through a credit facility from the World Bank (US$115m) and other donors, including DFID and the Japanese government.

It is clear, however, that the mere introduction of the private sector will not address the interests of the poor. Some civil society groups, principally ISODEC and its brainchild, the Coalition against the Privatisation of Water (CAP), have raised a number of concerns about the PSP process. Their main areas of concern are that:

- cost recovery, a feature of PSPs, will hurt the poor;
- the PSP process will favour only large foreign multinationals, and repatriation of profits from wholly cedi-based revenues will put pressure on the local currency; and
- there is no transparency in the PSP process and stakeholder consultations have been inadequate.

There have been no alternative proposals for undertaking the reforms, however, and everyone agrees reform is very necessary in view of the precarious water supply situation in the country.

Recent reports prepared in support of the investment programme by the World Bank have included pro-poor interventions such as standpipes and incentives to the operator to connect an estimated 50,000 poor households over the contract period. The UK's DFID is providing £8m in grant aid to the sector, and would like to see that their contribution addresses pro-poor interventions (Draft Project Appraisal Document, World Bank, 2004). In addition the PURC, in collaboration with the GWC and WaterAid, is undertaking pilot interventions aimed at addressing the water supply needs of the urban poor, with a view to both learning good lessons for replication and informing regulatory policy.

---

25. A significant observation is that different indications of coverage are provided by different organizations. This appears so because there is no national consensus on the definition of coverage. This raises the question of defining 'access' as well. For example, almost everyone in Accra depends on (and therefore has 'access' to) water produced by the GWC, albeit a substantial majority do so through secondary and tertiary providers. This is because there are few if any alternative sources. So Accra may be 80 per cent covered; but most poor people depend on SWEs with implications for prices paid and consequently quantities used.

26. The establishment of this Working Group has been delayed, due in part to the stalled processes in Ghana's water sector reforms. Recent indications are that a management contract agreement will be signed with an operator, in place of the previous lease arrangement.

27. Discussions with the Executive Secretary and the Chairman of PURC reveal that the Commission is contemplating requiring the utility to allocate a percentage of their production to tankers.

Chapter 11

Consensus-building and Opportunities for Partnerships

11.1 Stakeholders' workshop: Background

The stakeholder interface workshop to present the findings of this research was held on 20 May, 2004 at the Miklin Hotel Conference Room in Accra. The purpose of the workshop was to generate discussion on issues emerging out of the research and to synthesize ideas, with a view to formulating actionable strategies for remedying the operational and other constraints that SWEs face.

The workshop was attended by 36 participants drawn from some 10 stakeholder institutions (including SWE groups). Key institutions represented included PURC, MoWH, GWC, Water Resources Commission, GBC, NBSSI, WaterAid, etc. The Welcome Address was given by the Country Representative of WaterAid Ghana, Madame Aissa Toure.

The workshop consisted of presentations by the Project Team Leader (K.S. Manu) and the Lead Researcher (Dr K. Mensah Abrampah). A working group session looked at the key issues and attracted full participation from all present. Of particular interest and significance was the participation of two female vendors, who followed the proceedings and contributed through translations into and from their local languages.

The full report on the workshop as well as a list of participants is attached in Appendix 8. Below is a presentation of the key issues that came up at the workshop and the recommendations for a way forward in developing appropriate partnerships with SWEs to serve the poor.

11.2 Key issues

Key issues raised during the research were classified under the following headings: water supply, finance, water quality, and technology. These and the constraints presented were classified and discussed by participants under two broad headings:

(a) Operational/ Finance/ Capacity Building Issues and (b) Institutional/ Regulatory Issues (details presented in Appendix 8).

Water supply

For SWEs in Accra the only supply of potable water is the GWC. With the general inadequacy of supply experienced by all consumers, SWEs are also seriously constrained. Shortages resulting from such inadequacies, especially in the dry season, invariably push prices upward to the detriment of the poor end-user.

The general consensus of participants is that supplementary supplies from groundwater sources should be explored for tanker operators. It was noted that even though it is generally known that groundwater sources in Accra are saline, some areas around the city, such as Abokobi and Oyibi, are currently fed on borehole supplies with acceptable salinity. It was also noted that a more positive attitude towards SWEs can help ensure access to supplies.

Water quality

Water quality issues generated a lot of interest. Since there are no established quality assurance procedures along the supply chain neither vendors nor consumers are sure of the source and the quality of some tanker supplies. The research shows that their only means of assessing quality is through the colour, smell and taste of the water. For many vendors ensuring the quality of their water for customers is more crucial than any part of the business. Make one slip with this and you can lose all your customers. Yet vendors cannot check the source of the water neither can they really assess the hygiene status of the tanker. The issue of water quality hinges more on trust in the supplier and the keenness of the recipient.

Participants held the view that stakeholder institutions must provide the necessary remedies to the quality issues. It is expected that the PURC would play a lead role

---

Box 11.1. A vendor's complaint

'I have been a vendor for five years but just a month ago I changed my mind and stopped. This is because many of the tankers are not being truthful. The tankers deliver far less than the amount they claim to have delivered and the only means by which we are able to assess this is after selling and this always affects the expected profit margin. For some of them the quality of the water also cannot be vouched for. In order not to sell suspected water to households I just stopped. Until a means is established to regulate the water volume delivered and quality the business will continue to be unfair.'

Mr Ibrahim, Water vendor at Ashaley Botwe

---

in addressing this concern. Using the competencies of institutions like the FDB, the Standards Board, the GWC, District Assemblies and the Ministry of Works and Housing in ensuring tanker inspection, disinfection and certification could achieve this, according to participants.

Price of water
Another issue, which generated copious discussion, was that of the GWC tariff for tanker bulk supplies. It was noted that at current levels, the rates charged are above domestic tariffs. The case was made by tanker operators that as the ultimate end use is domestic consumption, they do not see the rationale in pricing their supplies above the approved domestic rate. Under the current dispensation the end-user is worse off since he is paying three main component prices:

- price for water (above domestic rate);
- tax (tanker operators pay tax to the Internal Revenue Service (IRS); and
- transport (which, it was argued, represented the pipes of the utility).

Some participants suggested that the GWC should consider pricing tanker bulk supplies below the domestic rate, and retrieving any losses to the utility through cross-subsidies from those who are connected to the mains.

11.3   Summary of key issues, constraints and strategies
Appendix 8 provides an elaboration of the main issues discussed and the strategies for addressing the constraints as identified by the report and by participants at the workshop. The issues include:

(a)   Water supply – improving the sources of supply to the SWEs to ensure fairness between those who are connected to the mains and those who are not.

(b)   Price of water – ensuring that the prices charged by SWEs are reasonable, not through price regulation but through arrangements that help to reduce their operating costs, e.g. bringing filling points closer to deprived communities, within the technical limits of the utility's operations.

(c)   Water quality – ensuring that the delivered water meets quality standards through regulation, monitoring, education, etc. at the various points of the distribution chain.

(d)   Financing – providing support to SWEs to finance their operations and to reduce their cost of capital.

(e)   Innovative technology and supply options – improving technology, particularly in the area of storage, and identifying alternative supply sources outside the traditional utility's.

(f)   Management capacity – building the capacity of SWEs (and CBOs) to manage their businesses or water supply.

(g)   Recognition – engaging all institutions to accept the role of SWEs and give them the appropriate recognition, understanding their constraints and providing them with needed support.

11.4   Viability of options for support to SWEs

Participants were requested to propose areas of intervention should Ghana be selected for Phase 2 piloting.

Areas for piloting Phase 2 interventions as proposed by participants are:

Exploring the possibility of mechanized boreholes to serve poor communities and to fill tankers

It is noted that the inadequacy of supply for tankers and the scarcity that results, especially in the dry season, puts negative pressures on end-user prices. It is thought that over-reliance on the traditional utility sources is the bane of SWE supplies. If consumers in the selected study communities are to get any relief, then alternative supply sources, such as boreholes, must be explored. Where sources of reliable groundwater do not exist in the communities themselves, such supplies could be sourced from other areas and trucked by tankers to supply vendors in the communities.

Use of community storage facilities for direct retail to end-users through the involvement of CBOs

Another supply arrangement as proposed by participants is the use of community storage facilities like polytanks to sell water directly to end-users. This is expected to involve CBOs who will make direct arrangements for tanker supplies with the tanker associations. It is expected under this kind of arrangement that since the CBOs will be dealing directly with the association and the utility, and not individual tanker drivers, prices will be lower. Similar arrangements have been tested between the utility and the tanker associations when private tankers are redirected – at the request of the utility – to other cities like Cape Coast and Koforidua to help alleviate supply shortages. In such cases, acceptable prices are discussed in advance and agreed and honoured by both parties.

Another advantage expected through this arrangement is that it will put the responsibility for tank disinfection and general hygiene in the court of the CBO.

Chapter 12

Proposal for Phase 2

12.1 Introduction

This proposal is a practical response to the issues that emerged from the research. It presents a viable and sustainable means of providing water to the urban poor. This is supposed to be on a pilot basis and should be able to be scaled-up if it works. The proposals from Ghana therefore present two key alternatives, with one focusing on a community vending system and the other on a tanker-based system. Both systems are aimed at responding directly to the key concerns identified in the research, and have been refined following the workshop in Dar es Salaam, where other participants' inputs were taken into account.

Key issues from research supporting pilots

Recognition

The concern of the SWEs was that they were not recognized by the GWC, PURC or policymakers. Operational arrangements are made between some tanker associations and the GWC but this does not give SWEs any influence on policies in the water sector. The PURC has initiated efforts to bring the SWEs into the policy milieu, but this effort is faced with major constraints given the lukewarm response of the utility. The SWEs have become a veritable alibi for the non-performance of the GWC, thus creating an obvious negative image for the SWEs.

SWEs are therefore craving recognition from policymakers, the GWC, and indeed the general public. This will take a concerted effort to attain.

Quality of water

The quality of water was a matter of concern for all the stakeholders in the water supply system. They agreed that the utility was responsible for the quality of water entering the distribution system. The quality problems occur during transport and storage. There is no established means to test water quality at consumption level. The two institutions who should regulate water quality – the Local Authority and Food and Drugs Board – do not have the capacity to do so. The storage facilities of vendors, tankers, and even household storage are all obvious places where water can become contaminated.

The desire is thus to institute measures and actions to ensure water quality at the transport and storage levels.

Supply of water
Accra's water supply level is about 40 per cent lower than demand, and given the inequality of distribution the case could hardly be worse for the poor. In the dry season the shortage affects the price and poor people pay even more. The tankers have to collect from further away, thus increasing the freight cost.

There is a need to develop alternative sources of water either through expanding the current source or by using other sources.

Operational cost
The operating costs for SWEs are quite high, especially for tankers, because they use very old vehicles. Vendors could also be experiencing a high rate of spillage and seepage from underground tanks.

There is a need to take action to reduce operating costs, and thus reduce the price of water.

12.2 Objective of proposal
In responding to these issues the proposals aim to:

- enhance the level of recognition of SWEs by other stakeholders, involve them in the development of policies for the water sector, and set the stage for greater collaboration among the stakeholders;
- improve the operations of SWEs so that they can reliably provide high quality water at a competitive price; and
- expand the water supply sources to ensure that the SWEs have adequate access to a sustainable source of water.

12.3 Proposal 1: Community-based bulk water storage system
This proposal is based on the dominant water chain systems that serve the poor as shown in Figure 12.1.

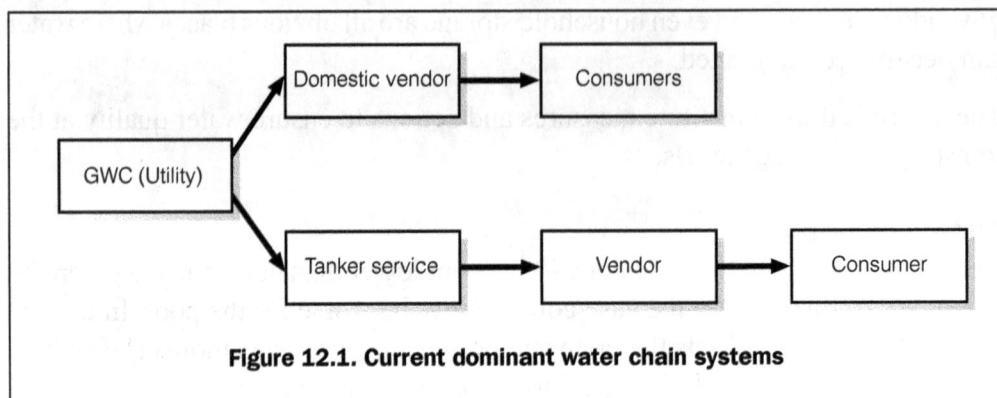

Figure 12.1. Current dominant water chain systems

The problem with the chain is that when water flows in some of the communities very little can be stored by households or domestic vendors. This creates shortages for the poor even when water flows within the week. On the other hand tankers have to drive long distances to transport the water and they spend a long time waiting to reach customers.

12.4 Strategy

To respond to this a three-pronged strategy has been adopted:

(a)   Undertake an advocacy process for SWEs to rescue and recreate the image of SWEs in the eyes of the public. This will involve:
   • Developing platforms for interaction among stakeholders
   • Publishing public outreach materials
   • Holding radio and television discussions on SWEs
   • Arranging fora with policymakers and law-makers on research findings
   • Advocating for SWEs to serve on water (decision-making) boards and committees

(b)   The provision of bulk water storage points where water from the GWC mains could be stored or bulk water from tankers could be discharged for a fee. The community would sign an agreement with a private operator to manage the facility. The bulk storage source could thus sell water directly to consumers, vendors and motorized cart operators, as shown in Figure 12.2

(c)   To ensure the quality of the water both vendors and households could be supported to acquire improved storage facilities. The bulk storage will ensure that a buffer supply is available, besides that supplied by the tankers. In areas where there are water mains, direct supply from the bulk water sources could be undertaken.

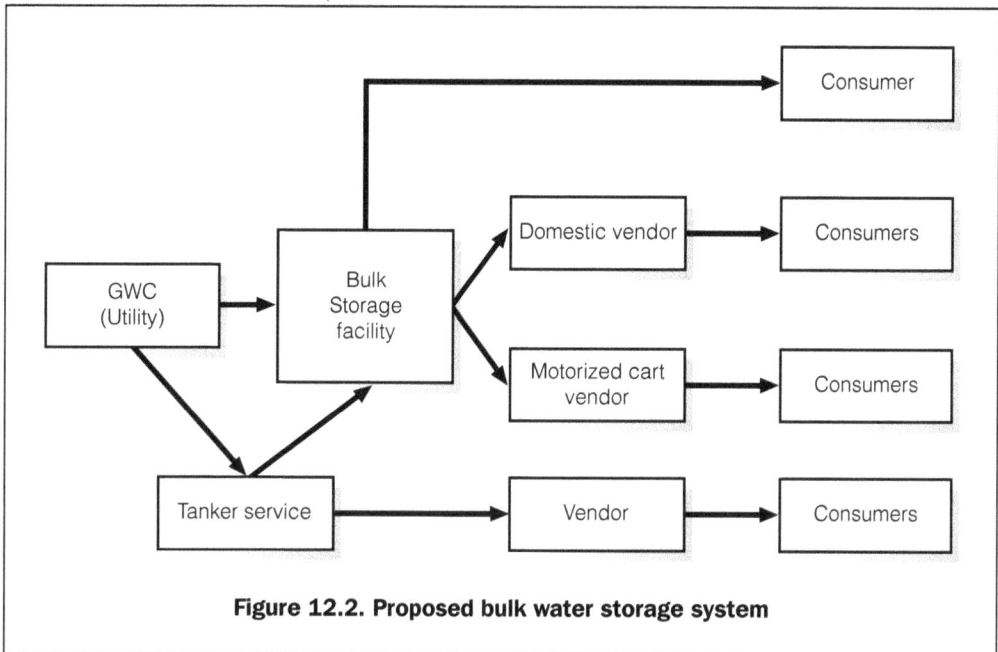

Figure 12.2. Proposed bulk water storage system

12.5 Roles

It is expected that WaterAid Ghana will undertake the advocacy activities, organization of vendors, and training in improving operational management. The community bulk water storage facility will be undertaken by the PURC and the GWC. It is expected that the WEDC project, together with the SWEs, will contribute in the provision of the improved storage facilities for the vendors and selected households.

Negotiations could be carried out with private suppliers to provide improved storage facilities on credit as is already happening. The guarantee would be provided by the project. It is expected that the research component regarding observations, data gathering, monitoring and reporting will be undertaken by WaterAid directly or sub-contracted to a consultancy firm.

12.6 Risk

The risk associated with the proposal is very minimal as the PURC and GWC are fully poised to undertake pro-poor activities and to learn lessons for addressing water supply provision to the urban poor.

The SWEs are very much prepared to offer all the needed support. Nevertheless the associated risk is that the funds from the expected key funders – the PURC, the GWC and WEDC (DFID) – do not appear.

12.7 Key benefits

The key benefits associated with the proposal are that:

- it will provide an opportunity for all the key stakeholders to interact in the pursuit of the project;
- the image and competence of the SWEs will improve;
- water costs for the poor will be lower;
- equity of access to water for the poor will be ensured;
- there will be a sustainable process for ensuring water quality; and
- the water will be cheaper for poor people.

Chapter 13

Conclusions and Way Forward

13.1   Water supply to the urban poor

The issue of water provision to the urban poor is receiving a lot of attention from public agencies – the Ghana Poverty Reduction Strategy Project, the Ministry of Works and Housing, the Public Utilities Regulatory Commission, and Ghana's Development Partners (the World Bank, the EU, development banks, etc.). There are more good intentions than actions so far, though. It is clear that many poor people will continue to depend on SWEs for their water supply needs for some time to come. The pace of reforms in the urban water sector, the investment profiles for the next decade, and the rate at which the city is expanding point to the fact that the water supply needs of many who are not connected to the mains will not be met in the near term. Reforms and PSPs will not in the immediate future outlaw SWEs from the distribution chain, and more innovative ways of engaging them to serve the poor should be sought.

13.2   Water supply challenge in Accra

Many people in Accra are not served by the Ghana Water Company because the piped network does not extend far enough, demand outstrips supply, and some people are unable to pay the high connection fees; as a result some poor consumers, even in areas that are part of the piped network, have to depend on neighbour sellers. The evidence that water supply coverage in Accra is around 80 per cent does not explain the supply choices available to consumers, particularly the poor. Many of them have to depend on secondary and tertiary providers.

13.3   Understanding the role of SWEs

Despite their acknowledged presence in urban water delivery, very little has been done in the way of understanding the role of SWEs, the constraints facing them, and the impact they make in addressing the needs of the poor. Small water enterprises – tankers, cart operators and domestic vendors – are playing significant roles as default providers. They are not given full recognition, however, and their activities have not been mainstreamed into the distribution chain until near normalcy in water supply through the utility can be achieved. In a number of cases they are seen as villains and profiteers who take advantage of the situation to exploit consumers.

13.4   SWE organization

Some SWEs – tanker operations in particular – are well organized and can be mainstreamed into the distribution system and properly monitored and supported. Domestic vendors, whose services are considered most reliable by poor consumers, remain unorganized, and in some cases are operating illegally in the view of the utility. Their operations raise questions about water quality.

13.5   Consumer perspectives of SWEs

There is considerable trust among those who depend on SWEs. The perception of trust and reliability in vendors is high, and is certainly stronger than any promises that they will receive water supply from the utility. Vendors' payment arrangements have also been noted to favour the poor.

Consumers dependent on SWEs pay up to 14 times the unit cost of water supplied by the utility to other customers who are in the same social tariff group. Obviously they do not use the same quantities of water and spend more of their income on water at the expense of other needs. What this indicates is that the poor could have the means and the ability to pay for services that are tailored to their needs and payment options. Studies of willingness-to-pay conducted in the last few years as part of Ghana's water sector reforms indicate a higher willingness-to-pay among people who are unserved or under-served.

13.6   Consumer opportunities

Some poor consumers have limited or no storage facilities for water and therefore do not enjoy the full benefit of the current rationing arrangement that the utility has embarked upon. On the other hand the proliferation of domestic vendors in a place like Teshie indicates that a community-owned and managed bulk storage arrangement that involves a partnership between the community, GWC, and the tanker associations could help reduce the overall price paid by poor consumers.

13.7   Stakeholder perceptions

Participants at the workshop were of the view that the utility has not been innovative enough in responding to the needs of poor consumers, and that they are more inclined towards high-profile engineering tasks. It was reported that one community in the supply area of GWC benefits from a borehole system that has reduced the price paid for water from ¢700 to ¢200 per bucket. This example could provide a lesson for replication.

13.8 Making SWEs benefit all

Many low-income people make money from water – either as direct retailers of water themselves or because they use it in other commercial activities. This implies that support to SWEs will not only improve access to those who do not receive service from the utility; it will also benefit those who depend on them for their livelihood.

13.9 Piloting interventions

A pilot scheme that addresses the water supply needs of low-income consumers through a community-managed bulk storage arrangement will bring prices down and impact positively on the poor consumers. The identification of alternate supply sources (as has been done by some SWEs in Kumasi and in Abokobi) ought to be looked into by the utility, instead of them relying solely on traditional project concepts. Participants at the workshop felt that the GWC is best suited to identify these alternative sources, as the Community Water and Sanitation Agency has done for Abokobi, a suburb that lies within the confines of the GWC supply area.

13.10 Forging partnerships

Lastly, it is pertinent to mention that the issue of service provision to the poor is not one for the utility alone to deal with. It requires the collaborative efforts of all agencies, the utility, the community, SWEs and NGOs. In the Ghanaian context, undertaking any scheme to address water provision to the poor will involve all or some of the institutions and players shown in Table 13.1.

Table 13.1. Definition of roles in scheme to provide water supply service to urban poor communities

	Institutional (sector) players and roles		Tasks/remarks
	Major	**Minor**	
Policy	MoWH, PURC	DA	Define social policy framework for the provision of water supply to informal, poor communities.
Strategy	All sector players (consultative) as undertaken at workshop		Identify issues and challenges and agree actions to be undertaken.
Funding	GoG	NGO, community, private sector (SWEs)	Any pilot projects shall be funded outside the current investment programme of the utility. Funding could cover capital works/equipment, community mobilization and training, subsidizing acquisition of storage, etc.
Community mobilization and sensitization	NGO (WaterAid)	Unit Committees / CWSA	NGOs are better placed for community development work. Lessons from community and small town water supply arrangements will be useful in this regard.
Service provision	GWC, SWEs		Utility should deliver bulk water, arrange regular supplies through SWEs, provide technical support including water quality management, and identify non-traditional sources of water, e.g. boreholes.
Training	Private training bodies	GWC, NGOs	Provide training needs of SWEs/CBOs in the areas of record-keeping, pricing, water-quality monitoring, etc.
Management	SWEs, Community		Management of the facility, whether through private sector, SWEs, CBOs or other groups.
Regulation	PURC	Accra Municipal Authority	Regulate activities of SWEs, particularly in the area of water quality and hygiene (PURC). Institute appropriate by-laws and regulations on hygiene, siting of facilities (Accra Municipal Authority), etc.
Monitoring and evaluation	MoWH, PURC, GWC	Consultative	M&E will assist in policy design, future planning, and drawing lessons for replication. Actual activities may be carried out by private consultant on behalf of institutions.

References and Bibliography

(See Appendix 1 for more details of relevant studies.)

Acolor, G. (2001) *To disconnect or not disconnect: The Teshie Hydrant Experience.*

Aryeetey, E. (2004) *Household Asset Choice Among the Rural Poor In Ghana.* Paper presented at the Authors' Workshop for the Project on 'Understanding Poverty in Ghana', organized by the Institute of Statistical, Social and Economic Research, University of Ghana and Cornell University. http://www.isser.org/Poor%20Household%20Asset%20Choice%20in%20Ghana%201.pdf

BiG/ASI (2002) *Socio-economic survey on water accessibility 2002.* Commissioned by PURC. Business Intelligence Group/Adam Smith Institute.

Brook, Penelope and T.C. Irwin (eds) (2003) *Infrastructure for Poor People: Public policy for private provision.* World Bank, Washington, DC.

Brook, Robert and Davila, Julio D. (eds) (2000) *The Peri-Urban Interface: A Tale of two Cities.* School of Agricultural and Forest Sciences, University of Wales and the Development Planning Unit, University College London

GSS (2000a) *Ghana Living Standards Survey Report 1998/1999,* (GLSS4). Ghana Statistical Service, Accra.

GSS (2000b) *Population and Housing Census: Preliminary Results.* Ghana Statistical Service, Accra.

GSS (2000c) *Poverty Trends in Ghana in the 1990s.* Ghana Statistical Service, Accra.

Globalis (undated) *Ghana: GNI- Gross National Income per capita,* http://globalis. gvu.unu.edu/indicator_detail.cfm?IndicatorID=140&Country=GH

GoG (2003) *Ghana Poverty Reduction Strategy, 2003-2005. An agenda for growth and prosperity.* <http:// povlibrary.worldbank.org/files/Ghana_PRSP.pdf> [23 Dec 2005]

ISODEC (1999) 'Kumasi Social Mapping Exercise Report for DFID Water Sector Improvement Project'. Unpublished Report.

Kunfaa, E.Y. (1999) *Consulting with the Poor. Ghana Country Synthesis Report.* World Bank, Washington, DC.

London Economics (1999) *Ghana Urban Water Supply: Demand assessment and willingness to pay study,* – Progress Report, February 12, 1999. London Economics and John Young & Associates, London.

Manu, K.S. (2001) *PPIAF/CWSA Study on Private Sector Participation in Small towns Water Supply.* Final Report. WSP. www.wsp.org/publications/sa_rwss.pdf

Macalester (Undated) *Map of central Accra* <http://www.macalester.edu/geography/courses/geog261/eskidmore/hotaaccra_map1.png> [23 Dec 2005]

Mensah-Abrampah, K.E. (1998) 'Challenges and threats to Communal coping strategies: the case of the poor and sustainable development in Ghana'. *Local Environment,* Vol.3 No.2, pp 137-157.

MIME Consult (2002) *Promoting the Development of Arrangements for the Provision of Services to the Urban Poor.* MIME Consult, Accra, Ghana.

MoWH (2004) 'Draft National Water Policy'. Ministry of Works and Housing, Accra.

Oguah, C. (2004) 'Personal communication with C. Oguah, Regional engineer, Accra Tema Metropolitan Area, (Accra West)'.

Owusu-Achiaw, K. (2002) *The Morphological Development of Accra and implication of Land uses.* SPRING Research Series 31, University of Dortmund, Germany.

PPIAF/CWSA (2002) *Development and Implementation of Pilot Projects involving local enterprises in small towns water supply and sanitation in Ghana.* Report by MIME Consult, Accra, in conjunction with the Community Water & Sanitation Agency (CWSA).

PURC (2002) *Socio-economic survey on water accessibility in Ghana,* Report by BiG/Adam Smith Institute, London, UK.

PURC (2004) 'Draft Guidelines for Tanker Operations'. Public Utilities Regulation Commission, Accra.

TREND Group (2000) *Ghana Case Study, Strengthening the capacity of water utilities to deliver water and sanitation services, environmental health and hygiene education to low income urban communities.* Water Utility Partnership (WUP Project 5). WUP, Abidjan, Côte d'Ivoire.

World Bank, (2004) 'Draft Urban Water Project Appraisal Document'. World Bank, Washington, USA.

Appendices

Appendix 1

Some relevant studies on water supply to urban poor people

There have been quite a number of studies on water supply in Ghana and particularly on urban water systems, but there are few that are relevant to the provision of service to low-income and urban poor communities. In addition not much work has been done on the role of SWEs. However there are a few studies that can provide some insight into the subject in the Ghanaian context. Some useful works in the area are:

a) **TREND (2000)** *Strengthening the capacity of utilities to deliver water and sanitation services: Ghana Case Study Documentation* commissioned by the Water Utility Partnership (WUP) to study the issues affecting the provision of water and sanitation and analyse the institutional potential and practices available for the specific case of the low-income areas. This was part of a wider project to detail case studies in the provision of water and sanitation services to poor and low-income communities in selected African countries. The study looked at a number of practices within Accra on the provision of services, including: (a) GWC–Tanker owners' metering/payment collaboration; (b) community-initiated private mains extension; and (c) individual vending from domestic taps.

b) **MIME Consult (2002)** *Promoting the development of arrangements for the provision of services to the poor,* which examined existing policy and institutional and regulatory arrangements for addressing the water supply needs of the urban poor. It was prepared to support the establishment of a consultative body to proactively look at how the urban poor could be catered for as the private sector was being invited into the operation and management of urban water supply.

c) **George Acolor (2000)** *Institutional arrangements for services to the poor: Some urban practices in Ghana,* which discussed the structuring of tariffs by GWC and tanker associations, as well as community mains extensions, and their impact on low-income/poor consumers.

d)   **ISODEC (1999)** *Kumasi Social Mapping Exercise,* which carried out a social mapping of Kumasi, the second largest city in Ghana, to identify low-income and poor communities, their accessibility to water supply, and, using participatory approaches, identified options by which their water supply needs could be met. The exercise was 'to help incorporate the concerns and needs of the poor and protect their right to the benefits of the investment' in the water supply expansion that was being considered at the time.

e)   **BiG/Adam Smith Institute (2002)** *Socio-economic survey on water accessibility 2002,* commissioned by PURC. The survey was designed to capture information to assist PURC in carrying out its mandate in (a) tariff regulation; (b) quality of service; (c) quality of the product; and (d) accessibility; and was undertaken by BiG, working in collaboration with the Adams Smith Institute (ASI). The survey covered over 3000 households (interviews) in selected GWC/PSP piped areas across all ten regions of Ghana, with particular focus on the poor.

In addition to the above documents, there are a number of sources which provide useful insight into the provision of water in urban areas, including various publications available from the Ghana Statistical Service (Accra, Ghana):

'Ghana Living Standards Survey 1998-1999',
'Poverty Trends in Ghana in the 1990s'.

Appendix 2

Names of key people contacted

Amengor, S.	Chief Manager, ATMA (Tema), GWC
Fosu, E.	Chief Manager, ATMA (Accra East), GWC
Oguah, C.	Regional Engineer, ATMA (Accra West)
Acolor, G.	Asst. Commercial Director, GWC
Nkrumah, E.	Co-ordinator, Project Management Unit, Urban water Restructuring
Adu, S.	Executive Secretary, PURC
Kotei, Nii	Director, Water Quality Inspectorate, PURC
Ofori, Maame Dufie (Mrs)	Director, Consumer Affairs, PURC
Cdr. Addo	Chairman, PWTOA
Osai,	Chairman, Lashibi Tanker Association
Ablorh, E.	Financial Secretary, Lashibi Tanker Association
Toure, Aissa (Mrs)	Country Representative, WaterAid
Nyarko, K.	Lecturer, Kwame Nkrumah University of Science and Technology
Alhaji Ibrahim	Vendor, Ashalley Botwe
George Mensah	Deputy Director of Town and Country Planning, Ministry of Environment Science and Technology, Accra
Parker Allotey	Public Relations Director, Accra Metropolitan Assembly
Angela Farhat (Mrs)	Programme Co-ordinator; Ghana Poverty Reduction Strategy (GPRS), National Development Planning Commission, Accra

Appendix 3

Information gathering guides

Guide for focus group discussions/participatory discussions

1. Let operators/vendors identify their catchment area (customers) on Map of the Community drawn by the group.
2. Obtain the key sources of their water and the reason for the source.
3. Discuss how prices are determined.
4. Use seasonal maps to discuss seasonal changes in the business and pricing.
5. Discuss whether there are any group activities/association activities.
6. Discuss the viability of the business (opportunities and constraints).
7. Discuss whether there has been an expansion/contraction in the business.
8. Discuss problems associated with the business.
9. Discuss the prospects and what could be done to improve the business.
10. Discuss their understanding of the ongoing reforms in the water business and how they will impact on their operations.

Questionnaire for tanker/cart operators

[The interview should be conducted by first explaining the purpose of the study and assuring the respondent that the information being gathered is not for tax purposes nor is it going to be used to drive them out of business].

i. Location: ....
ii. Driver's Name: (Optional) .... Vehicle Number: ....
iii. Name of Association ....
iv. Owner: ....
v. Date of Interview: ....

Vehicle Operating History

1. What type of vehicle do you use for the supply of water (specify type)? ....

2. What is the make and year of manufacture of your vehicle? ....

3. For how long have you used this vehicle as a water tanker /cart? ....

4. For how long has the vehicle been used for the supply of water in this area? ....

5. What is the capacity of your tanker/cart? ....

6. What are the major cost components in operating this vehicle?
   (e.g. fuel and lubricants; replacement of parts; replacement of tyres)
   i. ....
   ii. ....
   iii. ....

7. How much do you spend on the following daily/monthly?
   (Note: Be sure that the response is per day or per month)
   a. If owner operator

Item		Amount spent
i.	Fuel	....
ii.	Spares	....
iii.	Tyres (specify period)	.... (per ....)
iv.	General maintenance	....
v.	Driver's wages	....
vi.	Taxes, levies	....
vii.	Other	....

   b. If truck is rented, what is the charge per day ....

Customer/Client Service

8. Indicate the category and number of clients/customers you serve?

	Category	Number
a.	....	....
b.	....	....
c.	....	....
d.	....	....

9. How often do you supply water to your customers/clients? ....

10. Is there any arrangement with your customers/clients on payment terms?
(Explain how it works)
i. Water supplied and customer pays later? ....
ii. Customer pays in advance ....
iii. Water supplied and payment made in instalments? ....

11. What is your source of water? (Tick)
a. GWC mains
b. Boreholes
c. Hand-dug well
d. Other sources (specify) ....

12. Where are your sources of water/filling point (hydrant)?...

13. What is the average distance from your source point/filling point to the delivery point?
(state in km.) ....

14. What is the shortest distance between your filling point and delivery point? ....

15. What is the farthest distance between your filling point and delivery point? ....

16. How much do you pay for a full load of water (in cedis) from the following sources?
i. GWC mains
ii. Borehole
iii. Hand-dug well
iv. Other sources (specify) ....

17. How much do you sell a full load of water to the following?

Customer	Amount Charged by	Distance from Filling Point
Less that 1km	1km-3km	More than 3km
Domestic Vendors	....	....
Small-scale industrial users	....	....
Construction uses	....	....
Direct consumers	....	....
Domestic vendors	....	....

18. How is the pricing of water done?
i. Fixed by Association in agreement with GWC ....
ii. Fixed by the Association ....
iii. Based on availability, competition, season ....

19. Do you pay any taxes?

	Tax Agent	Amount	Purpose
i.	VAT	....	....
ii.	Income Tax	....	....
iii.	Special Levies	....	....
iv.	Dues	....	....

20. On the average, how much do you pay as taxes per day? ....

Internal arrangements

21. Describe the operating environment at the filling point? ....

22. Do you belong to any Association? Yes/No

23. If yes, for how long have you been a member of the Association? ....

24. Do you pay any dues to the Association? Yes/No
i. If yes, how much? ....
ii. If no, why? ....

25. How many members form the Association? ....

26. What does the Association do for you? ....

27. If you don't belong to any Association, how is your activity regulated? ....

28. Are you engaged in competition with other Tanker/Cart Operators? Yes/No

29. If yes, describe the nature of the competition ....

30. If no, are there any restrictive practices preventing new water enterprises from entering the water supply market? ....

31. What are the key constraints to your operation and industry? ....

32. Are you a tanker owner or driver? ....

33. If driver, how much are you paid per month? ....

34. If owner, how much do you get per day? ....

35. Do you have any other employment? ....

36. Is your business a sole proprietorship (one man business) or limited liability entity? ....

37. Do you keep records of your operations? ....
i. Financial records for accounting purposes
ii. Records on supplies to customers/clients
iii. Other records (specify) ....

38. How much do you spend on the following per day?
a. Food ....
b. Rent ....
c. Travelling and transport (T&T) ....
d. Utilities (electricity, water, telephone, etc.) ....
e. Children's school fees ....
f. Remittances ....

39. What arrangement have you got with the utility (GWC)? ....

40. How do you assess the services provided by the utility (GWC)? ....

41. How do you assess water quality? ....

42. When do you assess the water quality?
a. Before delivery .... B. After delivery ....

43. In what way can the services provided by the utility be improved?

44. To what extent are current water sector reforms likely to impact on your activities?

Questionnaire/interview guide for water vendors/neighbour sellers

[The interview should be conducted by first explaining the purpose of the study and assuring the respondent that the information being gathered is not for tax purposes nor is it going to be used to drive them out of business].

i.   Name of vendor: (Optional) ....

ii. Location of vendor: ....

iii. Date of interview: ....

1. For how long have you lived in this community? ....

2. What is your major occupation? ....

3. Indicate your sources of income? (Order by amount earned)
    i. Main source ....
    ii. Minor sources (Please rank according level of earning)
       a .... , b .... ,c ....

4. For how long have you been engaged in water vending? ....

5. How did you enter into this business? ....

6. Where did you get your start-up capital? ....

7. Indicate your sources of supply? (You may choose more than one and rank)
    a. GWCL mains ....
    b. Tanker service ....
    c. Cart services ....
    d. Rain harvesting ....
    e. Borehole ....
    f. Hand dug wells ....
    g. Others (specific) ....

8. What is the nature of storage facility you use for vending? (Please tick)
    i. Overhead tank ....
    ii. Underground reservoir ....
    iii. Other ....

9. What is the capacity of your storage facility? ....

10. How adequate is your storage facility in relation to the demand for your services?

11. How long does it take to empty your storage facility? ....

12. Indicate the seasonal variations in demand ....

13. How do you estimate the quality of the water supplied to you? ....

14. How do you estimate the quality of water you sell to your customers? ....

15. Is there any regulation of your activities and by whom? ....

16. What taxes, levies etc. do you pay? ....

17. Do you keep financial records of your operations? ....

18. Indicate the categories of customers you serve and proportion sold to them?

      Use   Percentage sold to them

a. Domestic users ....

b. Small-scale industrial users ....

c. Construction users ....

d. Others (specify) ....

19. What is the average purchase price of water?

      Size (Litres)   Amount (ϕ)

i. Per full truck load of water ....

ii. Per a drum of water ....

iii. Per bucket of water ....

20. How much do you sell water to consumers?

      Size   Amount (ϕ)

i. Per drum of water ....

ii. Per bucket of water ....

iii. Other sizes (specify) ....

21. Indicate seasonal changes with pricing ....

22. Do you have access to credit facilities? Yes/No

23. If yes give details in terms of:
a. Sources of credit: ....
b. Terms and conditions: ....
c. Other arrangements: ....

24. If no how do you finance your business? ....

25. Do you have other people assisting you? Yes/ No

26. If yes, indicate the calibre of people and remuneration if any.
a. Calibre of staff: ....
b. Remuneration: ....
c. How many are male/female? ....

27. If no, how do you cope with the task? ....

28. a. Does the number of customers change in the course of the year ....
b. If Yes, what caused it ....
c. How did you respond to it ....
d. Is this problem still pertaining or resolved ....

29. a. Do you have problems getting regular supply of water? ....
b. If Yes, does it come at particular times ....
c. What do you do in response to such situations? ....

30. Suggest ways of improving services of your supplies? ....

31. Suggest ways you could improve your services to consumers? ....

32. What do you consider as the threats to your business? ....

33. What do you consider as the opportunities to your business? ....

34. a. Do you belong to any vendor association or grouping ....
b. If Yes what do you gain from belonging to the association or group? ....

Questionnaire/interview guide for consumers

[Explain the purpose of the study, indicating that the results are intended to provide a better understanding of the operations of SWEs so that these could be possibly scaled up for the benefit of low-income people].

Household characteristics

1. For how long have you lived in this community? ....

2. Are you a tenant or landlord? ....

3. What is your family/household size? ....

4. How much do you spend on the following per day?
   i. Food ....
   ii. Rent ....
   iii. Travelling and transport (T&T) ....
   iv. Utilities (electricity, water, telephone, etc.) ....
   v. Children's school fees ....
   vi. Remittances ....

5. What is the working life of the family/household members like?
   (Indicate occupation and where they work) ....

6. What is the average time spent by each family/household member at home/day?
   1. .... 2. ....
   3. .... 4. ....
   5. .... 6. ....

Water use

7. What are your sources of water?
   i. Major source: ....
   ii. Minor sources: (Rank according to level of usage)
       a .... , b .... , c .... , d ....
   iii. Indicate if there are seasonal changes with the sources ....

8. How often do you get your water from the source?
   Source   Frequency
   Major source   ....
   Minor sources (List)   ....

9. Indicate the sources of your water and amount paid?

Source		Frequency (No. of days)	Amount paid (Weekly, daily, monthly) Max. Min.
a.	GWC mains	....	....
b.	Tanker	....	....
c.	Cart services	....	....
d.	Neighbour-seller	....	....
e.	Vendors (tankers)	....	....
f.	Well/borehole	....	....

10. Indicate the various uses to which your family/household put water?
    Activity/uses per week (Sunday-Saturday)   Estimated quantity
    (In 34 size bucket)

    a. ....
    b. ....
    c. ....
    d. ....
    e. ....
    f. ....

11. What is your assessment of the price you pay for water?
    i. Price is normal
    ii. Price is average
    iii. Price is too high

12. If you do not pay directly for your water how you do get water? ....

13. To what extent can you say that the water you get from the above sources is wholesome?

14. Will you prefer other sources of water as against what is presently available?

15. How do you store your water?
    i. ....
    ii. ....
    iii. ....

16. Does water storage constitute a problem to you? Yes/No

17. If yes what is the nature of the problem? ....

18. Do you have access to any financial support to enable you to purchase containers for water storage? Yes/No

19. If yes, indicate the following

Sources	Amount	Terms/conditions
i.	....	....
ii.	....	....
iii.	....	....

20. If no, how did you manage with your present containers? ....

21. If no, would you still recommend any improvement? ....

22. What is your view of the role of those who provide you with water? ....

23. Do you have any payment arrangements with your suppliers/vendors in the areas of:
    i. Credit sales
    ii. Advance payment
    iii. Advance delivery prior to payment
    iv. Extended payments
    v. Other arrangements (specify) ....

24. How can your water quality be improved? ....

25. Do you believe that the activities of SWEs should be regulated? . ...

26. In which areas should there be regulation? ....

27. What do you suggest be done to the price of water you pay? ....

28. To what extent do you believe that current water sector reforms will impact on your access to water supply? ....

Appendix 4

Institutional roles in the water sector

Table A4.1. Institutional roles in the water sector

Institution (Enabling legislation)	Purpose and key elements
Ministry of Works and Housing	The□ (urban and rural). The policy objectives are achieved through its agencies, the WRC, CWSA, GWC and the ad hoc WSRP.
Ghana Water Company (Act 310, 1965)	The main objects of GWC are to: • Provide, distribute and conserve water for domestic, public and industrial purposes. • Establish, operate and control sewerage systems in Ghana.
WSRS (PMU)	This is a transitional body charged with overseeing the introduction of private sector participation into urban water supply.
CWSA (Act 564, 1998)	The act establishing the Community Water and Sanitation Agency gives it the following functions: • Provide support to District Assemblies to promote the sustainability of safe water and related sanitation services in rural communities and small towns. • Enable the Assemblies to encourage the active involvement of the communities, especially women, in the design, planning, construction and community management of projects related to safe water.
Public Utilities Regulatory Commission, 1997	The specific responsibilities of the PURC in relation to water supply are, among others: • To provide guidelines on rates chargeable for the provision of utility services and to examine and approve rates chargeable for provision of utility services. • To protect the interests of both consumers and providers of utility services. • To initiate and conduct investigations into the quality standards of the services given to consumers. • To monitor standards of performance for provision of services. Under the act every public utility is required to make reasonable effort to provide safe, adequate, efficient and non-discriminatory service.
Ministry of Local Government and Rural Development	• Responsible for the policies and programmes for the efficient administration of local government structures. With the current emphasis on decentralization, most of these policies are carried out through metropolitan, municipal, and district assemblies. • Mobilize and negotiate for international funding for capital projects in the sector: this has in some cases involved water projects as part of urban renewal programmes which have a poverty reduction focus.

(Table continued on next page)

District Assemblies (Local Government Act, Act 462, 1993)	This act devolved a number of responsibilities and powers over the management of local affairs to DAs. These DAs have no responsibility over urban water; however the concept of community management of water supply in rural and small towns places considerable responsibility on the DAs to ensure that water facilities are managed well and in a sustainable manner. DA may delegate any of its functions as appropriate to any Town, Area, Zonal or Urban Council or Unit Committee or such other body or person it may determine.
Ghana Standards Board	These empower the Ghana Standards Board to set standards for drinking water quality, among other things. Actual enforcement and monitoring are the responsibility of PURC, however.
Town and Country Planning	
National Development Planning Commission (GPRS)	
Parliament (Constitution of Ghana, 1992)	The relevant provisions of the supreme law of the land to PSP in water supply include Article 17, which permits Parliament to, among other things, make 'different provision for different communities having regard to their special circumstances'. In addition Article 35 (3) enjoins the state to promote just and reasonable access by all citizens to public facilities and services, which would naturally include water utilities.

Appendix 5

Information gathering guides

Articles of Agreement made on the .... Day of .... Between the Ghana Water and Sewerage Corporation, ATMA, P.O. Box 1840, acting by the Area Director (hereinafter called the Corporation) on one part and the Lashibi Water Tanker Owners Association of c/o P.O. Box TN 71 Teshie, Nungua Est. (hereinafter called the Association) on the other.

Whereas the Corporation has undertaken to construct hydrant, which is metered, from which the Association shall draw water for the purpose of selling to the public, hereby agree:

1. That the Association shall abide by the code of conduct drawn by the Ghana Water and Sewerage Corporation;
2. That the code of conduct which is attached therefore forms part of this agreement;
3. That the Association shall make an initial payment of ¢500,000 as deposit towards drawing of water.

NAME ....   NAME ....
AREA DIRECTOR FOR AND ON BEHALF   FOR AND ON BEHALF
OF THE CORPORATION GWSC (ATMA)   OF THE ASSOCIATION

WITNESS..   WITNESS ....

NAME ....   NAME ....
AREA COMMERCIAL MANAGER-GWSC

CODE OF CONDUCT FOR PRIVATE WATER TANKER OWNERS ASSOCIATION
1. Only registered Association vehicles with GWSC shall be allowed to draw water.
2. The list of all such registered vehicles shall be made available to GWSC, ATMA with names of both owners and the drivers.
3. All registered vehicles shall bear the Association's Registration Number and the capacity shall be legibly written on both sides of the bulk.
4. All registered vehicles shall be subject to regular inspection to ensure that they are road worthy, clean and suitable for the delivery of water, by both parties.
5. The area around the hydrant shall be kept hygienically clean at all times. There shall be periodic inspection of the vehicles by both parties.
6. Rates approved by GWCL shall apply to all registered vehicles and be displayed at all the hydrants.

7. The Association shall pay an amount of 500,000 cedis (or an amount determined by GWCL) as an initial deposit for the commencement of drawing from the hydrant.
8. Business starts from 6:00 a.m. every day and ends at 6:00 p.m. the same day.
9. Meter shall be read by the appointed Meter Reader from GWCL and the Association's representative, bi-weekly.
10. Bill will be raised monthly and shall be paid by the first week of the following month, failure to pay by this date will result in immediate disconnection. Reconnection will be effected only after full settlement of amount due, together with a reconnection fee of Two Hundred Thousand cedis.
11. All drivers should be neatly dressed and be in proper footwear (no slippers allowed)
12. All drivers shall charge the approved GWCL rates accompanied by Waybills
13. Driving under the influence of alcohol or hard drugs is prohibited and any driver caught will be summarily dismissed.
14. Any driver who wilfully causes damage to the hydrant shall be made to bear the full cost of its repairs and workmanship.
15. All drivers should be courteous to both staff and their customers.
16. There shall be regular meetings between the Association and GWCL to discuss any problem that may arise.
17. The Company has the right to abrogate this agreement if it becomes necessary.

NAME ....   NAME ....
AREA CHIEF MANAGER FOR AND   FOR AND ON BEHALF
ON BEHALF OF THE COMPANY (GWCL)   OF THE ASSOCIATION

WITNESS...   WITNESS ....

NAME ....   NAME ....

Business starts from 6:00 a.m. every day and ends at 6:00 p.m.

Appendix 6

Reasons for choice of supply option

To learn why people choose one source of water over another a pair-wise ranking was used to rank the criteria based upon the consumers' own rankings. The pair-wise ranking indicates that the most essential criterion is reliability. This is very important for poor households, since many of them do not have storage facilities at home. This is followed by trust in the supplier, since this is an embodiment of the quality assurance and price arrangements essential for poor households who need to secure water when they cannot pay immediately.

Figure A6.1 also shows the ranking of preference criteria by GWC's mains-connected domestic customers in the study carried out BiG/ASI for PURC. The results are in very sharp contrast to the poor customers of the SWEs, who ranked 'convenience' lowest and 'reliability' highest (see Table A6.1). In both cases 'reliability' or 'ease of getting water' was ranked first. 'Payment scheduling' was

Table A6.1. Pair-wise ranking of criteria for consumer preference (Teshie)							
	Convenience	Quality	Reliability	Trust	Payment schedule	Unit of purchase	Total	Rank
Convenience		Quality	Reliability	Trust	Payment schedule	Unit of purchase	0	6th
Quality	Quality		Reliability	Trust	Payment schedule	Quality	2	4th
Reliability	Reliability	Reliability		Reliability	Reliability	Reliability	5	1st
Trust	Trust	Trust	Reliability		Trust	Trust	4	2nd
Payment schedule	Payment schedule	Payment schedule	Reliability	Trust		Payment schedule	3	3rd
Unit of purchase	Unit of purchase	Quality	Reliability	Trust	Payment schedule		1	5th

ranked third by consumers of SWEs (Table A6.1) while the 'cost of water' and 'accurate billing' were both ranked favourably (Figure A6.1). 'Contamination- free' water was ranked sixth (Figure A6.1) and 'quality of water' was ranked fourth (Table A6.1).

The obvious difference between the two groups of customers had to do with 'convenience', which was ranked lowest by the poor customers of the SWEs mainly because they claimed that if the water is available and the source is reliable any inconvenience will be tolerated. Customers thus travel a long way to reach reliable vendors and tankers in the lean season. For customers who rely on GWC mains services (usually to their house), searching for water outside the house is very inconvenient and 'time consuming'. It is thus not surprising that 'ease of getting water' was ranked first. It is a very important lesson that for the customers of SWEs, the poor households, reliability of supply is the most important factor while for GWC customers convenience is the key.

To analyse the preferences a matrix ranking was used for a focus group discussion, which revealed the matrix below (Table A6.2). Focus group members assigned weights to six different criteria, with greatest weighting (6) being assigned to 'reliability', indicating that this was considered to be the most important criterion.

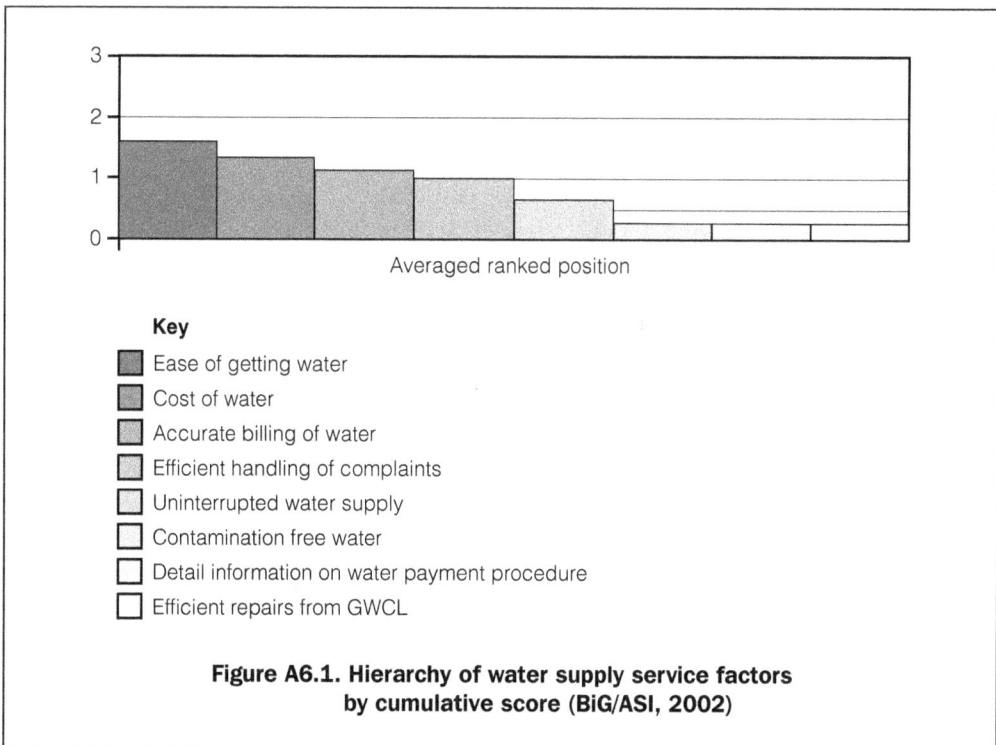

Averaged ranked position

Key

- Ease of getting water
- Cost of water
- Accurate billing of water
- Efficient handling of complaints
- Uninterrupted water supply
- Contamination free water
- Detail information on water payment procedure
- Efficient repairs from GWCL

Figure A6.1. Hierarchy of water supply service factors by cumulative score (BiG/ASI, 2002)

Source: BiG/ASI Survey – 2001/2.

Table A6.2.	Matrix ranking of criteria for consumer preference (Teshie)						
		Source of supply for consumers					
Criteria	**Weight**	**Vendors (Neighbour-sellers)**		**Motorized cart**		**Tanker**	
		No.	Weighted No.	No.	Weighted No.	No.	Weighted No.
Reliability	6	3	18	2	12	1	6
Trust	5	3	15	2	10	1	5
Payment schedule	4	3	12	1	4	2	8
Quality	3	2	6	1	3	3	9
Unit of Purchase	2	3	6	2	4	1	2
Convenience	1	3	3	2	2	1	1
Total			**60**		**35**		**31**

Consumers then assigned scores from three different sources of supply (vendors or neighbour-sellers, motorized carts, and tankers), ranking them from 1 (worst) to 3 (best). The weighted scores were obtained by multiplying the weight for each criterion by the ranking. Higher scores indicate increasing customer satisfaction.

Matching the ranked criteria to the sources it was obvious that the consumers preferred the services of the vendors. They ranked vendors highest for all criteria except quality, where they ranked tankers higher. Motorized carts were ranked second although water quality and payment schedule were both considered poor. There is a suspicion that some cart pushers collect water from ponds, and with respect to payment arrangements, which are crucial to the poor, cart operators were rated poorly because they often demand payment as the water is delivered. The cart operators are itinerant and therefore do not depend on fixed customers.

The discussion shows that consumers take into account a lot of very important factors in selecting their water supplier. The intended use of the water, the storage capacity of the consumer, and the disposable income of the consumer to a large extent influence the choice and the weight given to the criteria used in the selection.

Appendix 7

Workshop report summary

A7.1. Introduction

The stakeholder interface workshop to present the findings of the research was held on 20 May, 2004 at the Miklin Hotel conference room. The purpose of the workshop was to generate discussion on issues that were emerging from the research and to synthesize the ideas with a view to formulating actionable strategies for remedying SWE operational and other constraints.

A7.2. Participation

The workshop was attended by 36 participants drawn from more than 16 organizations and individual water vendors (including SWE groups). The full list of participants is attached within this Appendix.

Photograph © K.S.Mann (MIME Consult)

Photograph A7.1. Workshop participants

A7.3. Opening of the workshop

Chairman for the occasion was Wing Commander (RTD) Addo, Chairman of the Private Water Tanker Owners Association. He provided a brief background to tanker operations in Accra, outlined some operational challenges they face, and stressed the relevance of tanker operations vis-à-vis the current inability of the utility, GWC, to deliver acceptable levels of service to consumers in Accra. He stressed the importance of SWE roles and the need for mainstreaming SWE activities in urban water delivery. On this note he declared the workshop opened.

After a welcome address presented by the Country Representative of WaterAid, Aissa Toure Sarr, Kwabena Sarpong Manu, Executive Director of MIME Consult and manager of the research project, presented a briefing on the research project that covered water supply challenges and reforms, and policies and programmes, to address water supply to the urban poor. He also provided some relevant data on water accessibility, pro-poor issues, and a review of institutional roles.

A7.4. Presentation of the research findings

This was done by the Lead Researcher, Dr Kodjo Mensah-Abrampa. He took participants through the research objectives, methodology (including the criteria for research site selection), community characteristics, and the actual findings of the research. The findings of the research as presented include:

* a construction of the existing SWE supply chains in the project communities;
* a profile of price add-ons at different levels of the supply chain; and
* identified issues and constraints to SWE operations from the viewpoints of the various operators, etc.

A7.5. Discussions

Working Group Session

Key issues raised during the research can be classified under the following headings: supply, finance, water quality, and technology. The constraints presented were classified and discussed by participants under two broad headings: 'Operational/ Finance/Capacity Building Issues' and 'Institutional/Regulatory Issues' (see details in Table A7.1 and Table A7.2).

Water Supply

The only source of supply of potable water for SWEs in Accra is from GWC sources. With the general supply inadequacies experienced by all consumers, SWEs are also seriously constrained. Shortages resulting from such inadequacies, especially in the dry season, invariably push prices up, to the detriment of the poor end-user.

The general consensus of participants is that supplementary supplies from groundwater sources should be explored for tanker operators. It is noted that even though it is generally known that groundwater sources in Accra are saline, some areas around the city, such as Abokobi and Oyibi, are currently fed on borehole supplies with acceptable salinity.

Water quality

Water quality issues generated a lot of interest. Since there are no established quality assurance procedures along the supply chain, vendors and consumers are not sure of the source and for that matter the quality of some tanker supplies. The research shows that their only means of assessing quality is through sampling the colour, smell and taste of the water.

Participants held the view that stakeholder institutions must provide the necessary remedies to the quality issues. It is expected that the PURC would play a lead role in addressing this concern. Using the competencies of institutions like the Food and Drugs Board, Standards Board, GWC, District Assemblies, and MoWH to ensure tanker inspection, disinfection and certification could achieve this, according to the participants.

Price of water

Another issue, which generated copious discussion, was that of the GWC tariff for tanker bulk supplies. It is noted that the current rate charged is above domestic tariffs. The case as made by the tanker operators is that as the ultimate end-use is domestic consumption, they do not see the rationale in pricing their supplies above approved domestic rate. Under the current dispensation the end-user is worse off, since he is paying three main component prices:

- the cost of water (above domestic rate);
- tax (tanker operators pay tax to IRS); and
- transport.

Some participants suggested that the GWC should consider pricing tanker bulk supplies below the domestic rate. The participants' attention was drawn to the fact that domestic tariffs are highly subsidized therefore any such decision which does not take a careful account of the utility's production totals in relation to total tanker bulk supplies can make the utility worse off and therefore compromise sustainability. It was also noted that the water component of the tanker prices is less than 20 per cent, therefore the focus for cost cutting should be transportation rather than water.

Welcome address by Mrs Aissa Toure,
WaterAid (Ghana) representative at workshop

Stakeholder interface in the 'Study into better access to water in informal urban settlements through support to small water enterprises'

A welcome address delivered by the Country Representative of WaterAid Ghana, Aissa Toure Sarr 20 May 2004, Miklin Hotel – Accra

Mr/Madam Chairperson, Distinguished guests, Ladies and Gentlemen,

I wish to welcome you all to this workshop on behalf of WaterAid and its Partner NGOs operating in Ghana, the Ghana Water Company and WEDC. I believe for many of you this is not the first time you are participating and contributing to discussions on this study. Nevertheless, for the sake of our colleagues who are joining us for the first time, I would like to talk briefly about WaterAid and what it does.

WaterAid is an international NGO that works to help some of the poorest communities in Africa and Asia to provide themselves with a better quality of life through water, sanitation and hygiene promotion projects. Our vision is a world where everyone has access to safe water and effective sanitation.

In Ghana, WaterAid has been around since 1985 and has been providing technical and financial support to eight local NGOs to implement water, sanitation and hygiene services to poor communities in six regions in the country. The organization also takes a keen interest in research in order to promote informed and effective sector-wide decision-making.

Ladies and Gentlemen, the lack of access to safe drinking water is believed, and has been proven, to be a major cause of preventable poverty, diseases, and deaths in many third world countries. In Ghana, available data indicate that about a third of the population has no access to safe drinking water. This situation is even worse in the rural communities, where more than 50 per cent lack access to safe drinking water.

In the urban areas coverage levels appear better, with more than 70 per cent coverage. However, we have mostly tended to overlook the plight of the informal urban settlements that have no direct connections to the GWC main pipelines. Most of these poor settlers have, over the years, been taking advantage of the services of a number of small private water enterprises. Comparatively, these communities pay higher prices for water due to these intermediary services.

Since 2002, WaterAid and the Ghana Water Company, in collaboration with the Water Engineering Development Centre of the Loughborough University, have been studying the situation in Accra in order to find ways of improving the services of these small water enterprises so that they can in turn provide quality and affordable services to our poor clients.

MIME Consult has been our consultant for the project in Ghana and, after each phase, organizes a stakeholder interface so that all of us can also make our inputs.

We are here today to learn from the consultant how far we have gone with the study and, as usual, make our contributions in order to obtain a credible result that reflects the exact situation and the best suggestions that will help achieve our goals in the end.

I wish you all a fruitful discussion.

Thank you.

List of participants at workshop

Wateraid/wedc/gwc stakeholder workshop - 20 May 2004

	Name	Organisation
1	Esther Sekoh	Water vendor
2	C. Berkoh	Bhekans Ventures
3	Captain Victor Ansah	Cavacare Foundation
4	Agnes Arthur	Complan Consult
5	Joseph Acquaah	Complan Consult
6	Frederick Aye	Consumers Assoc. of Ghana
7	Marian Nanter	Gama Film Co.
8	Ama Kudom-Agyemang	GBC, Radio News
9	George Acolor	GWCL
10	Cynthia Ackah	GWCL
11	Dr George Botuhe	ISSER Legon
12	Dennis Vormawor	LET – Water Tanker Service
13	Paul Kukwaw	MIME/Complan
14	Atta Frimpong Manso	MIME Consult
15	Emmanuel Abankwa-Manu	MIME Consult
16	K.S. Manu	MIME Consult
17	Dr K. Mensah Abrampah	MIME Consult
18	W.B. Bortier	Ministry of Works & Housing
19	Abigail Kwashi	Ministry of Works & Housing
20	Huseini Mohammed	NBSSI
21	Samuel T. Ampittah	Private
22	Ms Millicent R. Mensah	PURC
23	Eric Obutey	PURC
24	Wg/Cdr C.O Addo (Rtd)	PWTOA
25	Celestina Deku	Town & Country Planning
26	M.A. Nashiru	WaterAid Ghana
27	Ibrahim	Water vendor
28	Magaret Nikoi	Water vendor
29	Aissa Toure Sarr	WaterAid Ghana
30	Emmanuel Addai	WaterAid Ghana
31	Ben Ampomah	WRC
32	Helen Essandoh	WSESP, KNUST

Appendices

Summary of issues, constraints and strategies (from workshop)

Table A7.1. Theme A: Operational/Finance/Capacity Building Issues		
Water supply		
Category	**Constraints**	**Strategies**
Tanker/Cart operators	• Old age of vehicles results in frequent breakdowns • Long waiting time at filling points • Insufficient filling points	• GoG must consider possibility of helping organized tanker associations to acquire good vehicles in the same way as it has done for other transport groups like the Ghana Private Road Transport Union (GPRTU). • GoG could consider waiving import duty on tanker vehicles. • Institute a revolving fund for tanker operators, to assist in maintaining and replacing vehicles. • GWC or tanker associations themselves should develop supplementary supplies from groundwater sources. • Tanker operators must be encouraged to form co-operatives and import inputs like tyres, batteries, etc. in order to get them more cheaply. • GoG must strive to improve the general economic conditions in the country, for example with low interest rates, etc.
Vendors	Supply backlog because tankers (for reasons above) cannot meet demand	• GWC should ensure good flow of water. • GWC reservoirs should be put to good use. • Water rationing should be properly done.
Price of water		
Category	**Constraints**	**Strategies**
Consumers		• Installation of community tanks into which tanker supplies could be delivered for direct sale to consumers. • Installation of community standpipes in poor communities for direct sales to consumers.
SWEs	High prices (tankers want to pay domestic prices)	• PURC must determine SWE prices. • Water sale to tankers must be priced either at or below domestic rate.
Domestic users	High prices per unit of measure	
Commercial users	High prices per unit of measure	

(Table A7.1. continued on next page)

Table A7.1. Theme A: Operational/Finance/Capacity Building Issues (*continued*)

Water quality

Category	Constraints	Strategies
Consumers	• Lack of public awareness of water quality	• PURC must take responsibility for SWE water quality assurance through periodic disinfection and certification of tankers through agencies like FDB or Standards Board.
SWEs	• Contamination • Using tankers to fetch raw water and for potable water	• Associations should develop mechanisms to ensure that members draw water only from their hydrants. • Inspection groups should be created to do regular hygiene inspections. • Vendors' storage facilities and general environment must be inspected periodically by town council health inspectors. • GWC could undertake regular disinfection of vendors' tanks for a fee. • Education of vendors and general public on water health issues through radio, television, etc.

Financing

Category	Constraints	Strategies
Tankers	• High initial investment • High maintenance cost • Lack of credit to beef up investments	• GoG must consider possibility of helping organized tanker associations to acquire good vehicles in the same way as it does for other transport groups like the GPRTU. • GoG could consider waiving import duty on tanker vehicles. • Institute a revolving fund for tanker operators.
Vendors		• Installation of community tanks into which tanker supplies could be delivered for direct sale to consumers. • Installation of community standpipes in poor communities for direct sales to consumers.
Consumers	• Difficulty in financing acquisition of adequate storage facilities • Lack of support for the water needs of the poor	• Installation of community tanks into which tanker supplies could be delivered for direct sale to consumers. • Installation of community standpipes in poor communities for direct sales to consumers.

(*Table A7.1. continued on next page*)

Table A7.1. Theme A: Operational/Finance/Capacity Building Issues *(continued)*

Technology		
Category	**Constraints**	**Strategies**
Tanker/Cart operators	• Unsuitable operations results in contamination of water	
Vendors	• Operational constraints (mode of water storage, means of drawing water by consumers, etc.)	• Design of vendors' reservoirs should be looked at to ensure that tap outlets are used instead of bailing out by means of buckets.
Consumers	• Use of bucket for storage • Contamination at filling points	
Management capacity/sustainability		
Category	**Constraints**	**Strategies**
SWEs	• Little or no record keeping especially in the case of vendors	• Training in book-keeping and basic accounting. NBSSI could take this responsibility. • Recognition of SWE role. The utility and other stakeholders must recognize the crucial role of SWEs. The necessary advocacy must be done by stakeholders like PURC, etc.

Table A7.2. Theme B: Institutional/Regulatory Issues (a number of issues already addressed under Theme A)

Water supply

Category	Constraints	Strategies
Tanker/Cart operators	• Insufficient filling points • Operational time limitations (4 days/ week; 12hrs/day) • Low volume of water (pressure problems)	• PURC and other stakeholders must establish some regulatory standards.
Vendors	• Supply backlog due to limited operational time of tankers	

Price of water

Category	Constraints	Strategies
SWEs	• GWC price to tankers perceived to be too high by operators	
Consumers – domestic/ commercial	• High costs trickle down to consumers	

Water quality

Category	Constraints	Strategies
Utilities/ regulator	Non-enforcement of water quality at: • Tanker filling points (hydrants) • Consumer s filling points (underground points)	
SWEs		• PURC and other stakeholders must establish some regulatory standards.

(Table A7.2. continued on next page)

Table A7.2. **Theme B: Institutional/Regulatory Issues (a number of issues already addressed under Theme A)** *(continued)*

Financing		
Category	**Constraints**	**Strategies**
SWEs	• Lack of formal arrangements for credit facilities	• National Board for Small Scale Industries (NBSSI) has indicated that they are ready to assist.
Tankers		
Vendors		
Consumers	• Lack of support for consumers water needs	• PURC and other stakeholders must establish some regulatory standards.

Recognition		
Category	**Constraints**	**Strategies**
SWEs	• Limited recognition of the role of SWEs in the water supply chain	National Development Planning Commission (NDPC) should re-examine and capture SWE issues in policy documents (e.g. GPRS). DAs should assume some critical interface for SWEs.

End notes

Chapter 1

1. In a recent PURC workshop at which the Project Leader was a participant, the PURC indicated that it was going to adopt a working definition of the urban poor as those:
    *   those without access to the utility's supply;
    *   who depend on secondary providers; and
    *   who purchase water by the bucket.

Chapter 2

2. This came out during discussions with the ATMA Chief Manager (Accra East) – 28th April 2004.

3. From discussions between Lead Researcher and Deputy Director of T&CPD, January 2004.

4. For a new connection, a customer makes two separate payments, the sum of which is higher than the cost of a direct connection to the utility's own mains (where this option exists). These payments are:
    *   fees to the CBO, after which permission is granted for connection; and
    *   the Ghana Water Company Limited new service connection fees.
    Poor people who reside in these areas are unable to make these payments and therefore cannot get connected.

5. According to the Project Management Unit for the Urban Water Sector Restructuring Project, the urban water sector requires a total investment of some US$1 billion over the next decade to bring total coverage to 85 per cent. So far the amount committed through the World Bank and other donors is US$150 million under the proposed five-year management contract.

6. These were provided for under the Draft Lease Contracts prepared in 1999/2000. Even though there has been a change to a management contract, there is no reason to believe that the pro-poor clauses will disappear in the new draft contracts.

7. Discussions with all three Regional Directors in Greater Accra revealed their preference for dealing with commissioned vendors, as the utility does not have the expertise to sell water at that level (through standpipes), and their experience in dealing with community organizations has not been good.

Chapter 4

8. It should be noted that because most properties in Ghana are generally owner-developed and financed, rather than purchased through estate developers or with mortgages, it takes a long time for houses to be completed.

Chapter 5

9. It should be mentioned here that the World Bank now uses the Gross National Income (GNI) and quotes $270 for Ghana in most of its documents (see Project Appraisal Document for Urban Water Supply Credit for Ghana, 2004).

10. Online discussion hosted by Nicola Tynan and Bill Kingdom on 'A Scorecard for Water Utilities in Developing Countries', Jan-Feb 2002. One could argue that the use of household income, rather than GDP per capita, is more appropriate, as there is only one water supply connection for the whole household. Note that the mean household income would be roughly twice as much as GDP per capita in the unlikely event that both spouses in a household may actually be earning income.

11. The sale of iced water in plastic sachets has come under tremendous attack in recent years because of its environmental impact. Accra city authorities have sought to impose a heavy levy on sachet water producers to enable them to clear the city of the plastic menace. This has met with considerable resistance and the city authorities have threatened to ban the sale of water in sachets. This would have tremendous impact on the livelihoods of a number of poor people, particularly women and children.

12. This came out in the focus group discussions and in the stakeholders' workshop as well.

Chapter 6

13. Based on discussions with ATMA Regional Manager, Accra East.

14. This is based on water quality analysis carried out by Esi Awua, a Senior Lecturer at the Kwame Nkrumah University of Science and Technology. The report is yet to be published.

Chapter 7

15. It must be noted that water supplied for construction activities is often collected from nearby ponds and not from the utility. This raises serious concerns for water quality. One association confirmed that some tankers do carry raw water to construction sites, thus compromising the quality of water purchased from GWC (as the next tanker load may be contaminated by polluted residue). However their members have been told not to do this, even though it is difficult to police the practice. This practice may also affect concrete quality for construction projects.

16. In deciding on the freight element of tanker-delivered water, reference is made to the guidelines used by the state institution responsible for the determination of national freight rates.

17. From discussions with the Chief Executive of the Labour Enterprise Trust, 20th May 2004.

18. Two coping strategies could emerge from this current arrangement. The first is that tankers go to places further away to collect water for their customers on the days they cannot collect from their regular filling point, and then charge substantially above the 'normal' rate. The second, which is not admitted by the Association, is that some tanker drivers may in fact use the truck to fetch raw water to serve construction sites, with serious implications for water quality.

19. One tanker operator, who at one point owned five tankers, now has only one and indicated that he has moved into the hospitality business because of the low returns in the water business.

20. In April, 2004 following a series of television reports on frequent water shortages at Sakumono, a middle-class estate near Lashibi, the GWC disconnected the filling point serving the Lashibi Tankers' Association. This led to a doubling of the rates charged to consumers dependent on their services, as they had to collect water from much further away. Following persistent counter outcry from the Association and a series of meetings with the utility, their activities were reduced to four days a week instead of the previous six days. Current rates are yet to reflect this new development.

Chapter 8

21. In the early 1980s the GWC decided to discontinue the use of public standpipes in the major cities and to shift demand to house connections due to a number of factors, including the difficulty of managing the standpipes (personal communication, Chief Manager, ATMA Accra East).

22. A vendor's costs will include amortization of the capital cost of the storage facility, salary/wages for the attendant, cleaning, and disinfection. Most vendors do not 'pay' themselves and do not see this as a cost.

23. During the interview with the Chief Manager (Accra East) he indicated that his office would soon go round to disconnect all vendors whose activities were affecting the flow of water to other residents.

Chapter 9

24. *Kenkey* is a popular local maize preparation that is consumed by both rich and poor, and is best taken with fish.

Chapter 10

25. A significant observation is that different indications of coverage are provided by different organizations. This appears so because there is no national consensus on the definition of coverage. This raises the question of defining 'access' as well. For example, almost everyone in Accra depends on (and therefore has 'access' to) water produced by the GWC, albeit a substantial majority do so through secondary and tertiary providers. This is because there are few if any alternative sources. So Accra may be 80 per cent covered; but most poor people depend on SWEs with implications for prices paid and consequently quantities used.

26. The establishment of this Working Group has been delayed, due in part to the stalled processes in Ghana's water sector reforms. Recent indications are that a management contract agreement will be signed with an operator, in place of the previous lease arrangement.

27. Discussions with the Executive Secretary and the Chairman of PURC reveal that the Commission is contemplating requiring the utility to allocate a percentage of their production to tankers.

www.ingramcontent.com/pod-product-compliance
Lightning Source LLC
Chambersburg PA
CBHW080250030426
42334CB00023BA/2767